AF412940

People in Profile
Christ Church Parish
1720-1750

By
**Katharine L. Brown
& Nancy T. Sorrells**

Historic Christ Church Heritage Books
Published by Lot's Wife Publishing for
the Foundation for
Historic Christ Church
P.O. Box 24
Irvington, Virginia 22480
2002

Cover design by Cheryl Lyon

Lot's Wife Publishing
P.O. Box 1844
Staunton, VA 24402

Library of Congress Catalog Card Number 2001099485
ISBN 0-9676027-7-7

TABLE OF CONTENTS

Foreword

A rhythm and pattern of life orbited around Christ Church in its earliest days. A mosaic of diverse souls struggled, prospered, failed, succeeded. Some acquired land and chattel. Some were indentured servants or slaves, having little or nothing to call their own. The stuff of life was accumulated, documented, used, abandoned, or passed on to heirs. Imprints were left on public records.

By examining court records, deeds, diaries, inventories, patents, processioners' returns, rent rolls, wills, and other primary sources, much has been learned about the people of Christ Church Parish in the first half of the 18th century. On these pages representative samples of Parish residents are profiled. Through the profiles a sense of the circumstances, stratification, and tempo of society in the parish emerges.

The book is based on the research work of the Parish Profile Committee of the Foundation for Historic Christ Church. The foundation and the members of the research team are indebted to Ann Dorsey, chairman of the project, for her vision, her leadership, and for the unflagging energy and attention to detail that guided the team to the completion of this portion of the project. Composed of dedicated, trained volunteers, the committee has poured over a vast assemblage of primary resources, identifying and documenting the people of the parish, their origins, occupations, possessions, relationships, and other notable circumstances. The committee includes Joan Alford, Mary Kay Davies, Ann Dorsey (Chairperson), Leila Ermarth, Charlotte Henry (who authored, as well as researched, the Edwards and Swan profiles), Carolyn Jett (who provided training and guidance in research methodologies), Marcus Key, Dixie McCaig, Dickson McKenna, Robert McKenney, B. J. Norris, Sue Rogers, Joyce Scott, and Virginia Wagener.

Ann Dorsey, Dixie McCaig, and Sue Rogers assisted the authors as readers, carefully critiquing the working drafts. The project has benefited from unique, significant contributions by all members of the committee. Publication of this volume is a benchmark in the Parish Profile Project, but not its end. The present committee members are also quick to acknowledge they are building on four decades of work done by previous Christ Church research volunteers.

The project benefited considerably from the resources and assistance of the Lancaster County Circuit Court Clerk's Office, repository of Lancaster County records dating from 1651, and the Mary Ball Washington Museum & Library.

Great praise is due Lot's Wife Publishing Company in the persons of Katharine Brown and Nancy Sorrells, who served as consultants to the project, as well as authors. They have been keel, ballast, rudder, and wind in our sails for the publication of this book, as well as the other three volumes in the series.

The foundation is deeply appreciative of the confidence and encouragement of the trustees and staff of the Jessie Ball duPont Fund. A grant given by the duPont Fund financed the Parish Profile Project, publication of this book, and its three companion volumes.

Robert A. Cornelius
Executive Director

ACKNOWLEDGMENTS

This small volume grew out of the desire to taste in the printed word some fruits of many years of digging and pruning in the research vineyard. In the course of their project to trace all the landowners and land boundaries in Christ Church Parish in the year 1750, the Parish Profile Research team at Historic Christ Church has collected a considerable body of material about persons who lived in the parish in the 18th century.

Research materials that have resulted from the project are being stored in the archive files in the Foundation for Historic Christ Church Library. The files include family information, abstracts of deeds, photocopies and transcripts of wills and estate inventories, court order book references, cross-referencing, and summaries about individual persons. It is an impressive resource that provided the basic information for this book. In the endnotes for these biographical profiles, FHCCRF is the abbreviation we have used for Foundation for Historic Christ Church Research Files.

The researchers had talked of "cameos" or biographical sketches of various persons in the parish. When the Foundation for Historic Christ Church engaged Lot's Wife Publishing to work with the researchers to produce four publications, a volume of such sketches was one that everyone found appealing. The researchers, staff, and publishers agreed that such a volume should attempt to include "all sorts and conditions of men" [and women] in the words familiar to those colonists from their *Book of Common Prayer*. Even though the research project focused on landowners, the majority of parish residents in the 18th century were not landowners. They were women, children, slaves, indentured servants, overseers, craftsmen, and tenants. Nonetheless, much information was accumulated about them through their ties and dealings with landowners.

The researchers suggested the subjects of these biographical profiles. They had collected the resources from which the profiles could be written and provided us wise counsel in the course of our writing. One researcher, Charlotte Henry, wrote two of the profiles, Mary Swan and Thomas Edwards, so that we only had editing and endnote work to do. Another, Marcus

Key, traveled to the Library of Congress to take notes from and about Robert Biscoe's 18th-century book.

Many persons around the Commonwealth aided this endeavor. The staff members at the office of Constance L. Kennedy, Clerk, Lancaster County Circuit Court, were unfailingly courteous and helpful in our work to locate and photocopy documents. Del Moore and other members of the Rockefeller Library staff as well as members of the Historic Trades departments at the Colonial Williamsburg Foundation assisted in locating materials and illustrations for the Biscoe, Anderson, and Banton profiles. Edmund Berkeley of Special Collections at the University of Virginia's Alderman Library and his uncle, Francis Berkeley of Charlottesville, kindly gave permission for the citation of Francis Berkeley's edited transcripts of the letterbooks and diaries of Robert Carter. Hill Carter of Shirley Plantation allowed the use of a photograph of Robert Carter's portrait. The library staff at the Mariners' Museum provided helpful material about small vessels as well as illustrations, which we used with their permission. Camille Wells kindly shared observations about her work at James Gordon's house, now called Verville, and about 18th-century architecture in general. Our attorney in Staunton, David McCaskey, cheerfully clarified some legal terminology. We are grateful to Professors Alan Briceland and Philip Schwarz of Virginia Commonwealth University for suggesting us to the Foundation to help with the parish profile project. Project member Dickson McKenna drew an elevation of the glebe house from descriptions for remodeling found in the vestry book for Christ Church and St. Mary's White Chapel Parish. Carolyn Jett read an early draft of the Gordon profile and offered suggestions.

In addition to all the members of the parish profile research team indicated in the Foreword, we wish to give special thanks to those who served as readers of several drafts of this book, and offered their very helpful suggestions: Ann Dorsey, Dixie McCaig, Sue Rogers, and staff member Robert Teagle, Education Director. Mimi Beckwith started this project on its way when she was Executive Director, and her successor, Bob Cornelius, has been a constant supporter and wise advisor.

Katharine L. Brown	**Staunton, Virginia**
Nancy T. Sorrells	**March 2002**

VIII

Edwin Conway
Virginia Burgess

Robert Carter, (1663-1732), builder of Christ Church, whose wealth and power earned him the nickname "King," was unquestionably the dominant figure in Christ Church Parish, in Lancaster County, and even in Virginia during the first half of the 18th century. Edwin Conway (1681-1763), however, was a more representative example of the planter class that dominated the political, economic, and religious life of the colony. Conway exemplifies the English colonists who settled Tidewater Virginia and brought English institutions — county government by landed families, the established Church of England with its strong local parishes, and a representative form of colonial government. Conway served all three institutions as a justice in Lancaster County, a vestryman for Christ Church Parish, and an elected representative to the House of Burgesses in Williamsburg, the Virginia capital.

Those who rose to wealth and power in Virginia in the latter part of the 17th century were from a small circle, often of gentry background in England, who established strong ties in Virginia through marriages. Edwin Conway, Lancaster County's longtime Burgess, was the third generation in Virginia to bear the name. His grandfather, probably from Worcestershire,[1] married Martha Eltonhead of Lancashire about 1640. Her sister, Agatha Stubbins, already in Northampton County on Virginia's Eastern Shore, may have encouraged the Conways to settle there. That Edwin Conway was clerk of the Northampton County court from 1642 to 1648.[2]

Martha Eltonhead Conway's sisters Agatha,[3] Alice, Eleanor, and Jane, in their successive marriages into prominent planter families like Wormeley, Chichley, Carter, and Corbin, exemplified the network of kinship ties developed among Virginia's late 17th-century planter elite.[4]

Edwin and Martha Eltonhead Conway had a son, Edwin,

born about 1644 and a daughter, Eltonhead, about 1646. Around 1650 Edwin Conway decided to move his family to the western shore where his Eltonhead sisters-in-law had married so well. In December 1652, he received 700 acres in Lancaster County for transporting 14 persons to Virginia, including his wife, Martha.[5] A 1657 patent brought 1,650 acres that remained in the family.[6]

The young Conways grew up on the Northern Neck in a circle of the elite of Chesapeake society. They were niece and nephew to Sir Henry Chichley and cousins to the Wormeleys and to John Carter's sons, John and Robert Carter. John Carter, builder of the first Christ Church in Lancaster County, made a deed in 1656 to his "niece Eltonhead, the Daughter of Edwyn Connaway," giving her a cow.[7] Their uncle, William Eltonhead, an associate of Capt. Henry Fleete of Lancaster County, became a member of the Maryland council and bestowed gifts on Edwin and Eltonhead.[8]

In 1678, after Edwin Conway I died, his son, Edwin II, received 1,650 acres that his father had patented in 1657. Edwin Conway II married Sarah Walker, daughter of Col. John Walker, Esq. of Gloucester County and his wife, Sarah, the widow of an Eltonhead family friend, Col. Henry Fleete.[9] Through marriage and purchase, Edwin Conway II acquired nearly 3,000 acres in Rappahannock (later Richmond), Essex, and Middlesex Counties.[10] Edwin Conway II was trained as a surveyor. In 1688, when Accomack and Northampton Counties had a boundary dispute, the governor dispatched Conway to this area where he had been born to run the boundary line between the two counties.[11]

Edwin Conway III, the subject of this biographical sketch, was born in 1681. His mother, Sarah Walker Conway, had died by 1695 when his father married Elizabeth Thornton, by whom he had a son, Francis, in 1697. In 1695, Edwin Conway II made out a deed of gift to his son, Edwin, and daughter, Mary, with Henry Fleet II and the Reverend Andrew Jackson, minister of Christ Church Parish, as trustees for the two minor children.

Edwin III received the Lancaster plantation where his father lived, a plantation occupied by tenants, and 1,000 acres south of Indian Cabin Swamp. Mary received a 550-acre tenanted plantation north of the Indian Cabin Swamp (in Wicomico Parish), so long as she did not marry before February 16, 1702. Edwin also received a slave girl, Ann, and a slave boy, Thomas, four cows, a silver tankard, three silver spoons, his father's gold rings, and a stone ring that had belonged to his mother.[12] This deed of gift indicates that the family owned accouterments of gentility.

Edwin Conway III was only 17 when his father died in 1698, leaving behind his three children and a pregnant widow, for whom he would provide very well. Edwin Conway II's will, probated in Richmond County in September 1698, confirmed the 1695 deed to Edwin III and Mary. Edwin also received "all and every part and parcel of my estate in Lancaster County, not before given, except one negro man named Jack," and "my bay Mare, and *all my wearing cloths*, and all my mathematical instruments and bookes, and all the cloth and stuff sent for to England, when please God they doe arrive." Conway named four overseers (administrators): his kinsman, Henry Thacker,[13] the minister, Andrew Jackson, Samuel Fox, and his young son, Edwin. In accordance with his will, Conway was probably buried "in my burying ground in Lancaster, by the left side of my dear wife *Sarah*, dec'd, at the discretion of my Brother-in-law, *Mr. Henry Fleete*, and *Mr. Andrew Jackson*."[14] This practice of many Virginia planters, large and small, of having a family burying ground on their own land explains in part why there appear to be so few burials in the churchyard of Christ Church.

Edwin Conway III first appears on the Lancaster County tithable list of 1700. Taken annually for the county levy, the list included each male head of household, along with other white males over the age of 16 and male and female slaves aged 16 and over. In Christ Church Parish there were 119 heads of household. Only six men had more than 10 tithables, with Robert Carter heading the list with his 84. Thirty men had only themselves to account for, 25 had only two tithables, and 28 had three. Thus, 83 men, or 70 percent of the parish, had three or fewer tithables. Conway, young and single, with four tithables, had more labor at his disposal than the great majority of men in the parish.

In 1704, at the age of 23, Conway married Ann Ball, a daughter of Col. Joseph Ball (1649-1711) and Elizabeth Romney Ball (c.1653-1703). Ann Ball was the older half-sister of Mary Ball, who married Augustine Washington and became the mother of George Washington. The Ball family of St. Mary's White Chapel Parish was one of the most prominent in Lancaster County, filling important positions on the county court, the vestry, and in the militia.[15] Some economic benefit may have come to Conway in this marriage, for Joseph Ball may have settled some land, slaves, or money on his daughter, as was customary with planter families, but no marriage settlement document survives to verify this. Mary, the sister of Edwin Conway II, as a widow married Major James Ball in 1707.[16]

After Ann Ball Conway died, Edwin married Ann Hack, probably the granddaughter of a Dutch couple, Dr. George Hack and Anna Hermann [Varlett?] Hack, who had immigrated to Virginia and patented land in Northampton County in 1652. Dr. Hack became a denizen, a limited citizenship status for aliens.[17] Besides practicing medicine, Hack was a ship owner who traded tobacco with the Dutch colony of New Netherland (New York).[18] Dr. Hack's 1665 estate inventory included 22 German and Dutch books, 54 in Latin, and 20 in English, an unusually large library for the time.[19] Col. Peter Hack, the Accomack-born son of George and Anna Hack and father of Ann Hack Conway, settled in Northumberland County, Virginia, adjacent to Lancaster County, where he was a vestryman in 1712 and sheriff from 1716 to 1717.[20]

Conway was the father of eight children born between 1705 and 1727: Elizabeth, Anne, Mary, Agatha, Peter, George, Hannah, and Millicent. The first four were probably the daughters of Ann Ball Conway. Named for her father and grandfather, the two sons, Peter and George, were the children of Ann Hack Conway, as were the two youngest daughters, Hannah and Millicent.

Most of the Conway land holdings were on the Corotoman Neck of Christ Church Parish, between the eastern and western branches of the Corrotoman River. A patent that the first Edwin Conway had for 2,500 acres in this area was sold early and became the property of the William Tayloe family, whose members were related to the Conways through the Eltonhead marriages; however, some of this later came back into Conway ownership. From time to time Conway added to his landholdings. In 1711 he traded two slaves for 200 acres south of Indian Cabin Swamp.[21] In 1729 Conway purchased 382 acres from John and Elizabeth Thornbury for £500 sterling.[22] In 1748 Conway deeded 1,000 acres to his son and heir, Peter, while retaining his own life interest in 500 acres.[23] It is likely that this tract included the old Conway home and family cemetery. It was later the county poorhouse site and currently encompasses the Hickory Hollow Nature Trail. Conway purchased 212 acres of his grandfather's large patent from his cousin, John Tayloe, and then deeded it to James Gordon who married his youngest daughter, Millicent.

In 1722, as part of an effort to ensure the quality of Virginia tobacco, the General Assembly passed a law requiring the construction of tobacco "rowling" or rolling houses. The Lancaster County Court, in carrying out its provisions, ordered the construction of four rolling houses, only one of which was in Christ Church Parish. That was to be built "on the Land of Edwin Conway Gent at the head of the Western branch of the Corrotoman River." That waterway was navigable to within a mile from the present Lancaster Court House. Conway maintained a right-of-way for his rolling road leading to the landing where the tobacco house was located.[24]

In 1743 the long dissatisfaction with the location of the courthouse at the failed town of Queenstown opposite the Carters' Corotoman plantation led to the decision to move it to a

Memorandum

The two acres of Land whereon the new Court house Prison Pillory Stocks & whipping post are erected for the publick use of this County which s.d two acres were given by Edwin Conway for that purpose are bounded as followeth Viz.t Begining at a stake near the S.E corner of the prison and runing N 25° E 24 poles or an half and three Links of a chain to a stake close on the N.E side of the main road thence up the s.d road N 65° W 13 poles to another stake on the same side of the road thence crossing the s.d road S 25° W Paralel to the first Course & the same distance to a stake by the woods thence S 65° E 13 poles to the begining.

Ordered that three acres of Land begining at the N.W corner of the Court house Land & runing N 65° W 19½ po thence S 25° W 24½ po & 3 Links thence S 65° E to the S.W corner of the Court house Land thence to the begining which s.d three acres belonging to Peter Conway together with the two acres of Court house Land are hereby appointed for the Rules of this County prison and it is further ordered that Peter Conway forthwith cause to be set up Chestnut posts to mark out the bounds plainly of y.e s.d rules for the use of prisoners according to Law

In 1743 Edwin Conway donated two acres of land for the relocation of the Lancaster County courthouse. The courthouse remains in the same vicinity today. (Courtesy the Mary Ball Washington Museum and Library)

more central site. For that purpose Conway donated two acres where the county militia had customarily held its monthly muster. The new courthouse, prison, pillory, stocks, and whipping post were erected there. The site is now occupied by the Mary Ball Washington Museum and Library and the old jail across Route 3 from the present courthouse. The bounds of the tract were recorded on March 10, 1743. The courthouse built at that site was used until the construction of the present one in the mid-19th century.[25]

No trace remains of the Conway house on the entailed land that grandson Peter Conway inherited. Furthermore, it is not certain where Edwin Conway was actually living at the time of his death. His will stated, "I give to my Grandson Edwin Conway my Dwelling House and Plantation Together with all the Lands and their appertenances which I hold in fee simple."[26]

Conway's inventory, taken in 1764 after his death at 82, probably reflects the possessions and configuration of the plantation in the 1740s and 1750s, when he was still an active justice, vestryman, and Burgess in his sixties. The house, most likely frame, had grown over the years from a center block of four rooms, two down — the hall (a main room where the staircase was located), and the parlor — and two rooms up, that could have been a story-and-a-half or even two full stories. A chamber with a closet and loft "the Room and Col. Conway's Room loft" were likely additions, and the room designated "the New Room" clearly was added later. The kitchen could have been attached by the area designated "the Passage." Conway's furniture included seven beds with their bedding, seven tables, 63 chairs, six chests, one desk, two corner cupboards, and five looking glasses, most listed as large.[27]

Conway had four tithables in 1700 shortly after he came into his inheritance. In 1746, after his children had all married and left home, Conway had 15 tithables. The slaves were Bachus, Daniel, Harry, Stephen, Tim, Joe, Grace, Kitty, Sarah, Ned, Moll, Fairweather, Bess, and Solomon. No indication survives of their ages. In 1762, when Conway made out his will, 16 slaves can be accounted for. Daniel, Harry, Stephen, Ned, and Moll were still there. One of the 1746 women must be by 1762 "the old blind woman whom I desire may be kindly used as Long as she shall Live," but it is impossible to say whether that was Grace, Kitty, Sarah, or Bess. His ratio of two men to one woman remained constant, even though the individuals changed.[28]

The first of the Conway children, Elizabeth, had married Christopher Garlington in 1724 before the last two children were born, Hannah in 1724 and Millicent in 1727. In 1724 Anne married Robert Edmonds and Mary married Thomas Gaskins of Northumberland County. In 1737 Agatha married Cuthbert Spann. Peter married first Elizabeth Spann and then Elizabeth Lee. George married Ann Heath of Northumberland in 1739. Hannah married Tunstall Hack, probably a cousin, in 1746 when she was 22, and Millicent, the youngest, married James Gordon, a recent immigrant merchant-planter from the north of Ireland, in 1742 when she was only 15.[29]

In 1710, Conway began a political career in the House of Burgesses. It was somewhat unusual in Virginia for a planter to sit in the House of Burgesses before he became a justice of the county court, but Conway only became a justice in 1720, serving in that capacity until 1750. He represented Lancaster County in the sessions from 1710 to 1718, and again from 1723 and nearly every session from then until 1755, a total of 40 years. Frequently, one of the members of the Ball family of White Chapel Parish was the other Lancaster County Burgess serving with Conway. Of the 168 men who served in the House of Burgesses between 1688 and 1776, no other member met or exceeded Conway's record. Conway took a break from the House of Burgesses in 1748 and 1749 when he was appointed Sheriff of Lancaster County.[30] In those years his son, Peter Conway, was elected to the House of Burgesses.

The number and importance of committees on which Conway served in the sessions of 1712, 1715, 1730, 1732, 1734, and 1752 would not justify calling him one of the most powerful Burgesses. However, his committee service in the sessions of 1736, 1738, 1740, 1742, 1744, and 1746-1747 placed him in the top ranking among the colony's lawmakers.[31] Conway's attorney, in arguing a suit, expressed his public role well when he stated that Conway

> hath for Sundry Years past enjoyed Particularly the Honour of being a representative of the Freeholders of the Sd County in Several General assemblies where he Has been Distinguished for His abilities & Faith-

fulness & often chosen to Preside as Chairman of Sundry Committees always exercising His utmost Industry care & Knowledge in Discharging His Duty to His Constituents by Strenuously Contending To Maintain the Rights & Pledges Liberty and Property of the People...[32]

In his early years in the General Assembly, Conway became an opponent of Governor Alexander Spotswood. In 1715, Spotswood was forced to call an assembly to appropriate aid for South Carolina following attacks there by the Yamasee Indians. The election results turned against Spotswood, with only 16 Burgesses retaining their seats. Those 16 included some of Spotswood's most notable opponents, among them Conway. Spotswood concluded the short and difficult session by delivering to the Burgesses a speech that was a "masterpiece of haughty invective." Spotswood told them "The Giddy resolves of the illiterate Vulgar in their Drunken Conventions you hold for the most Sacred Dictates to your proceedings," insulting both the Burgesses and their electors back home in one stroke, and mentioning three Burgesses by name, Edwin Conway, Gawin Corbin, and George Marable.[33] By the time the 1720 elections took place, Spotswood and the Council had resolved most of their differences. Twenty-two members of the House of Burgesses were not re-elected, among them Conway and Marable. This was Conway's only electoral defeat, for he was back in the House of Burgesses within three years.

Conway kept his finger on the political pulse in Lancaster County. Beginning in 1727, Joseph Carter, tobacco inspector at Corotoman, became the target of complaints about his temper and his administration of the duties of his office.[34] This sentiment came to a head in 1732 when William Gooch was governor. A persistent depression in the tobacco market had defied the efforts of Governor Spotswood to control tobacco quality through a patronage-based system of tobacco inspectors that was widely resented in Virginia. His successor had no more success with a stint law, which forced a production limit on planters. Under Gooch's skilled political leadership, the Assembly enacted a tobacco inspection law in 1730 with full approval of the Board of Trade in England and principal London merchants. Gooch had to overcome strong initial opposition to an inspection act in the House of Burgesses. Edwin Conway led that opposition.[35]

Conway is reputed to have made a fiery speech in 1732 at a muster held in Lancaster County. The targets of his anger were a recent act of Parliament forbidding planters to strip and stem tobacco prior to shipping it to England and the inspection act that required the burning of inferior tobacco. Conway's speech is said to have stirred local planters so much that they marched on the tobacco inspection warehouse at Corotoman and burned it.[36] Conway's own account of the matter survives in a letter he wrote to Governor Gooch on October 9, 1732, and casts him in a conciliatory light.

> I pacified the People last Tuesday at the muster by telling them that the Secretary had promised to hear their complaints, for several were ready to strike Mr. Carter, for he had been very partial and unjust, as the people say, and it may be proved that the other two were, for the most part governed by him. . . . The Inspectors passed very bad Tobacco for some people, and often burnt good Tobacco, and made the people pick it over and over again, &c., Mr. Carter has declared in the presence of several men, that he will be more severe in burning Tobacco if he continues Inspector another year. . . . Many people were desirous to give their evidence before the Secretary, but it is so far to Wmsburg & two great rivers to cross, the people so poor, and money so scarce, that unless the evidences could be examined here, 'tis better to carry our Tobacco to some other Inspector, for by Mr. Carter's Character he is a man of Implacable temper and we dare not carry our tobacco to him. . . .[37]

Conway saw himself as a champion of small planters in

this struggle with the hated tobacco inspector, a person against whom he had no objection until he saw him in action. While the great planters generally favored this law, small planters feared that different standards would be applied to different classes, and that they, less able to produce consistently large quantities of the highest quality tobacco, would see much of their tobacco burned by the inspectors.[38] Conway wrote another letter to Governor Gooch the next day urging that Joseph Carter not be re-appointed and expressing his hope that the governor would permit depositions to be presented detailing Carter's misdeeds. Conway also indicated that he feared that Mr. [Thomas] Edwards and Mr. Richard Lee and the Minister [probably the Rev. John Bell] would use their influence with the Secretary (John Carter, son of Robert Carter of Corotoman) to gain Joseph Carter's reappointment.[39] Resistance to renewal of the inspection act in 1734 was so strong on the Northern Neck that in the 1735 election, many incumbents who backed inspection were unseated. Conway, who was in the minority that retained their seats, was in a strong position when the Burgesses met in 1736. The House voted to repeal the inspection act, but the Council refused to accept the measure.[40]

There was no newspaper in Virginia when Conway addressed the Lancaster militia, but by 1736 William Parks had established the *Virginia Gazette*. Conway availed himself of this opportunity to express political opinion when he wrote a letter to the editor in April 1737, which was published as "A Hint to discover a few of Col Spotswood's proceedings." In this lengthy letter Conway reviewed the relations of Governor Spotswood with the Assembly from 1711 to 1720. He pointed out concern that Spotswood had subverted basic rights and privileges of Virginians and criticized his lavish spending on furnishing the Governor's Palace in Williamsburg. But the heart of his complaint was that Spotswood delayed until 1736 turning over arms intended for Brunswick County for which funds were appropriated in 1720. By Conway's calculation, Spotswood profited financially on such a deal.[41]

Col. Spotswood, by then retired to his "enchanted castle" estate at the site of the 1714 Germanna settlement on the Rapidan River, used his young son John to form a clever reply. The boy sent a letter to Parks.

> I have learnt my Book, so far as to be able to read plain English, when printed in your Papers, and finding in one of them my Papa's name often mentioned by a scolding man called Edwin Conway, I asked my Papa, whether he did not design to answer him. But he replied: "No, child, this is a better Contest for you that are a school Boy, for it will not become me to answer every Fool in his Folly, as the Lesson you learned the other day of the Lion and the Ass may teach you." This Hint being given me, I copied out the said Lesson and now send you the same for my Answer to Mr. Conway's Hint from
> Sir, your Humble Servant
> John Spotswood

Then followed an Aesop tale of an Ass "Mopping and Braying at a Lion" who responds by telling the ass to "Jeer on and be an Ass still, take notice only by the way, that, it is the baseness of your Character that has saved your Carcass."[42]

Conway continued his battle against the Tobacco Inspection Law in 1738, sending another letter to Parks for his *Virginia Gazette* that was published in November 1738. Conway said that "The express Instructions of *my Constituents* are to do my Endeavours to *Repeal* the law for *Inspecting Tobacco*" and that he would be failing his oath as a Burgess if he assented to the law. He argued that existing laws against false packing should be sufficient, and that the uneven and unjust enforcement of the Inspection Law caused great hardship to ordinary planters.[43]

Conway's desire to have a clear record of public service extended to his bringing suit against Thomas Pinckard, a local planter, in Lancaster County Court in 1745 on a charge of trespass. He engaged a lawyer, Cavan Dulaney, whose brief claimed that on January 23, 1743, through "False Scandalous

& Malicious words," Pinckard had exposed Conway to "the Contempt & Hatred of the People of the sd County" and attempted "totally to Destroy His good name, Fame and reputation" and brand him and his posterity "with everlasting and Indelible Infamy and Disgrace." Pinckard was alleged to have said "The People have found out Old Conway now, & therefore will choose Him no more." Venting further "Malice, Hatred & spleen," Pinckard on December 29, 1743, claimed, "I can prove Conway a Lyar and He has Deceived the People that chose him Burgess but now there Eyes were open." Then on February 11, 1745, Pinckard was heard to say, "Old Conway is a Damn'd Old Rogue, & Hypocrite, & He Deceived the People."[44] Dulaney asked damages of 100 pounds current money. The jury found for Conway but awarded him only £10. Pinckard and his attorney, William Kennon, appealed, but after losing the appeal in Lancaster County, they carried it on to the General Court in Williamsburg. The records of that body have been lost, so we do not know the outcome of the case. If Pinckard hoped to work toward unseating Conway, he failed, for the perennial Burgess continued to represent the county until 1752.

Conway was proud of his service in the Burgesses, pointing out in a letter to the editor in 1752 that he had served in 24 sessions "and never was detain'd one Day, in the whole Time, from the Service of the House, by Sickness or Lameness."[45] His purpose in the letter was to object to a proposal that the capital of Virginia be moved from Williamsburg to a site on a navigable river 50 miles west. His lively interest in political issues stayed with him even though he had retired from all secular political offices by 1752.

A devoted member of the Church of England, Conway served on the vestry of Christ Church Parish from 1739 until at least 1751. The surviving vestry book for that period deals mainly with St. Mary's White Chapel and only includes occasional joint meetings of the two vestries to deal with matters common to both, such as a major remodeling and expansion of the glebe house and outbuildings in 1744. Thus it is difficult to gauge Conway's activity.[46] When a Presbyterian congregation formed in Lancaster County in 1757 and announced its intention of building a meeting house, Conway was a leader in the opposition. In March 1758, the Lancaster County Court recorded its "prohibition against building a meeting house for Presbyterian Dissenters in the County."[47]

By early in 1759, Conway had been persuaded to drop his opposition. His former son-in-law, Col. James Gordon, an Ulster-Scot from the north of Ireland who was a leader in that Presbyterian group, visited the elderly Conway on January 9 and recorded in his diary that "The gentleman has now fully dropped opposing the meeting house, which is mostly occasioned by a letter he lately received from Mr. Ben Waller, who advises that the Dissenters have power to build a house and enjoy their religion by act of Toleration." Gordon visited Conway in May and exchanged some sharp words about a business affair. He confided to his diary, " I find his friendship to me is much lessened."[48] One can only wonder if some of this came from the religious differences, as well as the business affairs.

Conway did not relinquish his position easily, for in July 1759, Gordon noted that he "received a letter from Col. Conway, & one to Nancy upon religion, but in my opinion very little to the purpose. Thos. Carter rec'd one that displeased him very much. Col. Conway seems so great a bigot that people who are religiously inclined despise his advice."[49]

By 1763 Conway, now at age 82, was in declining health. James Gordon, who brought the new Presbyterian minister, James Waddell, to dine with Conway on April 1, 1763, commented that the old gentleman "seems much impaired, & will allow anybody to speak very little in his presence."[50] In September, Gordon reported a visit to the very ill Col. Conway, "who seemed pleased to see me." On October 4, Gordon recorded that "Col. Conway departed this life early this morning," and two days later he and his wife attended the funeral of the old Burgess.[51]

Conway had planned carefully for his departure from this mortal life in the will that he wrote in July 1762. He stated that he wanted the Reverend David Currie, minister of Christ Church Parish, to read his funeral service, and he provided for his executors to pay 40 shillings to Currie for doing so. However, Conway specified that he did not wish to have a funeral sermon preached. In reaching the advanced age of 82, Conway had outlived not only his two wives, but also most of his children. Although his grandson, Peter Conway, was his "heir at law," another grandson, also Col. Edwin Conway, was his executor. That younger Edwin's brother, Walker Conway, was an heir, as was another grandson, George Conway. Grandsons Joseph and Edwin Garlington received £30 current money, granddaughters Agatha Conway and Anne Conway, received slaves, and granddaughter, Agatha Eustace, received some furniture.[52]

For all his occasional irascible qualities, Conway was an excellent example of the planter gentry who brought English institutions and values to Virginia and nurtured them there. He passed from the scene before the stirrings of revolution had come to the colony, but he lived long enough to see and regret the forces of change in the appearance of a popular and growing dissenting denomination close at hand and even in his family, one that would undermine the very parish institution that Conway so faithfully served.

ENDNOTES

[1]Several genealogies of the Conway family are available to researchers but none provides much documentation. An article, "Conway Family," in *William and Mary College Quarterly; Historical Magazine*, series 1, 12(1903-1904):264-265, claims that he was "of county Wigorn, that is county of Worcester."

[2]Ralph T. Whitelaw, *Virginia's Eastern Shore: A History of Northampton and Accomack Counties*, Volume One (Richmond: Virginia Historical Society, 1951), 154.

[3]Agatha and Ralph Wormeley had two sons, William and Ralph. The latter survived and continued the Wormeley line. In 1649, Richard Kemp, Secretary of State for the colony of Virginia, patented 3,500 acres for transportation of 70 persons assigned to him by Ralph Wormeley. These included Mrs.

Agatha Wormeley, although it seems clear that Ralph Wormeley did not import her to Virginia, for she was in Northampton County with her first husband, Luke Stubbins, unless she returned to England following his death, married Wormeley there, and returned to Virginia. Nell Marion Nugent, *Cavaliers and Pioneers: Abstracts of Virginia Land Patents and Grants, 1623-1800*, (Richmond: Dietz Printing Company, 1934), I:182.

[4]By 1645 Conway's brother-in-law, Stubbins, had died. Agatha Eltonhead Stubbins' marriage to Ralph Wormeley of York County occurred after this. Wormeley had died by 1653 when Agatha married Sir Henry Chichley, who moved to the Wormeley plantation on Rosegill Creek (this part of York County later became Middlesex County). Martha's sister, Alice, had married Rowland Burnham of Lancaster County (this land is no longer part of present-day Lancaster), then after his death, Henry Corbin. Will of Rowland Burnham of Rappahannock in Virginia, 12 February 1655/56, Family Archive Viewer, *Virginia Colonial Abstracts*, Volume I, Lancaster County Record Book no. 2, 1654-1666 (Broderbund Software Inc., 1998). Bequests to Alice Eltonhead Burnham included all his silver plate (hollow ware) and £70 sterling. Eleanor Eltonhead married Capt. William Brocas, Esq., member of the Council in Virginia and a successful early planter in present Middlesex County. As a widow, Eleanor Brocas married Major John Carter of Corotoman and moved to Lancaster County. Darrett B. Rutman and Anita H. Rutman, *A Place in Time: Middlesex County, Virginia, 1650-1750* (New York & London: W.W. Norton & Company, 1984), 54; Jane Eltonhead married first Robert Morson of Kecoughtan Parish, Virginia, and secondly a Marylander. "Conway Family—Notes to Eltonhead Chart." Horace E. Hayden, *Virginia Genealogies. A Genealogy of the Glassell Family of Scotland and Virginia* (Wilkes Barre, Pa., 1891, reprinted Baltimore: Southern Book Company, 1959, Genealogical Book Company), 229-230.

[5]Nugent, *Cavaliers and Pioneers*,1:271.

[6]Edwin Conway I joined with a widow, Hannah Mountney, to patent 1,650 acres in Lancaster County for transporting 33 persons. Ibid., 1:359. See Patent Book 4:216, Library of Virginia.

[7]"Conway Family," *William and Mary College Quarterly; Historical Magazine*, series 1, 12 (1903-1904): 264-267; "Conway Family," *VMHB*. John Carter to Edwin Connaway for his niece Eltonhead the oldest heifer with all her increase both male and female at the plantation of William Lucas on the south side of the Rappahannock River. 9 April 1656. Lancaster County Deed Book 2:151.

[8]Capt. Henry Fleete to Wm. Eltonhead 1646, Archives Division, Virginia Sate Library, Northampton County, Deeds Wills, etc. No. 3, 1645-1651, Family Archive Viewer, *Virginia Colonial Abstracts*, Volume II, King and Queen County, Records Concerning 18th Century Persons, 5th Collection, Broderbund Software, Inc., 1998. Rutman, 49, 256 n.23, citing Lancaster Deeds, 1652-1657, 90-94 for examples of Eltonhead gifts to the Conway children.

[9]Henry Fleete was a militia captain in the 1640s when he is first associated with the Eltonhead family, but by 1656 he had advanced to lieutenant colonel.

[10]"Conway Family," Hayden, *Virginia Genealogies: Glassell*, 226.

[11]A letter from Edwin Conway II dated 22 March 1687/88 detailing his commission; the negotiations and the line drawn is reprinted in Whitelaw, *Virginia's Eastern Shore*, I, 38-39. Details on the political background of this

boundary dispute are discussed in Sarah S. Hughes, *Surveyors and Statesmen: Land Measuring in Colonial Virginia* (Richmond: Published for the Virginia Surveyors Foundation, Ltd. and the Virginia Association of Surveyors, Ltd., 1979), 13.

[12]The text of this deed is printed in "Conway," Hayden, *Virginia Genealogies: Glassell,* 234.

[13]Henry Thacker was the husband of Eltonhead Conway Thacker, sister to Edwin Conway II.

[14]Will of Edwin Conway, written 19 March 1698 and probated in Richmond County Court on 7 September 1698. Transcribed in Hayden, "Conway Family," *Virginia Genealogies,* 231.

[15]Thomas L. Broun, "The Ball, Conway, Gaskins, McAdam and other Kindred of William and Jenetta Broun of Northern Neck, Va.," *William and Mary College Quarterly; Historical Magazine,* series 1, 20(1911):60.

[16]"Conway Family," *William and Mary Quarterly; Historical Magazine,* 12:265.

[17]A denizen was an alien admitted to citizenship, but who could not hold public office or inherit land.

[18]Susie M. Ames, *Studies of the Virginia Eastern Shore in the Eighteenth Century* (Richmond: The Dietz Press, Publishers, 1940), indicates that a tobacco shipment from Dr. Hack to Cornelius Steenwick was received in good condition, citing Northampton County Wills & Deeds, 9 (1657-1666): 27.

[19]Whitelaw, *Virginia's Eastern Shore,* I: 684-688.

[20]See "Excursus-Hack," in Hayden, *Virginia Genealogies: Glassell,* 243-244. From the information provided here about the emigration of this Dutch couple to Northampton County, and birth of two sons on the Eastern Shore, then their subsequent naturalization in Maryland in the 1660s, it seems apparent that the second wife of Edwin Conway III could not have been the daughter of this couple. They were contemporaries in Northampton County of Edwin Conway I, the immigrant, who possibly knew them. Anna Herman Hack, wife of Dr. George Hack, was a sister of Augustine Hermann, a founder of the Bohemia Manor settlement in Delaware in 1669. It is more likely that the second wife of Edwin Conway III, Ann Hack, was the daughter of Col. Peter Hack of Northumberland County. Edwin Conway III was a witness to the consent of Col. Peter Hack to the marriage of his son, John Hack, in 1719. It seems likely that by this time, Edwin Conway was son-in-law to Col. Peter Hack. Peter Hack married Elizabeth, the daughter of Captain David Fox and Ann Wright, his wife. See also Whitelaw, I: 688-689.

[21]Edward Sanders to Edwin Conway, 21 September 1711, 200 acres in precinct E of Christ Church Parish that had been patented by Edward Sanders, grandfather of the grantor, in 1662 and 1669. Lancaster County Deed Book 9:361.

[22]John and Elizabeth Thornbury to Edwin Conway, 10 September 1729, Lancaster Deed Book 12:115. Elizabeth Thornbury was the daughter of Joseph and Barbara Tayloe whose land the Thornburys sold.

[23]Edwin Conway, grantor, to Peter Conway, grantee, 29 June 1748. Lancaster County Will and Deed Book 14:210.

[24]Lancaster County Order Book 7:68-69, 10 October 1722. According to FHCC researchers, this landing at the site of Conway's tobacco rolling road and house was still shown on a survey plat recorded in 1804. Lancaster County

Estate Book 1796-1806, 301-302.

[25]FHCC researchers discovered a memorandum regarding the gift from Edwin Conway of two acres and an additional three acres from his son Peter Conway that makes it possible to plat the land. Lancaster County Deed and Will Book 14: 10, 9 March 1743.

[26]Edwin Conway will, written 27 July 1762, proved 20 January 1764. Lancaster County Deed and Will Book 17:30.

[27]Edwin Conway inventory, taken 7 October 1763, recorded 20 January 1764. Lancaster County Deed and Will Book 17:31.

[28]1746 tithable list, Precinct F, Christ Church Parish; Edwin Conway will.

[29]"Conway Family," *William and Mary Quarterly; Historical Magazine*, 12:264 267; "Conway Family," *VMHB*; and Hayden, *Virginia Genealogies: Glassell*, 221-290, 238-247 esp.

[30]The four who came closest were Peter Pressley from Northumberland, who served 1710 to 1712 and 1715 to 1747, Charles Carter of Cleve, 1734 to 1764 from King George County, Lemuel Riddick 1736 to 1768 and 1769 to 1775, from Nansemond, and John Robinson II, 1727 to 1765, from King & Queen. Jack P. Greene, *The Quest for Power: The Lower Houses of Assembly in the Southern Royal Colonies, 1689-1776* (Chapel Hill, N.C.: Published for the Institute of Early American History and Culture at Williamsburg, Va., by the University of North Carolina Press, 1963), 463-474; *Executive Journals, Council of Virginia*, 5, (1 November 1739-7 May 1754), 259.

[31]Greene, *The Quest for Power*, 463-474.

[32]Edwin Conway, gent. vs. Thomas Pinckard, gent. Lancaster County Court Order Book 9 (1743-1752): 64a.

[33]Leonidas Dodson, *Alexander Spotswood, Governor of Colonial Virginia, 1710-1722* (Philadelphia: University of Pennsylvania Press, 1932), 129-130.

[34]Joseph Carter was a son of Thomas Carter II, and grandson of Thomas Carter, the immigrant, of Barford on the Corrotoman River near Merry Point. Carter was appointed Tobacco Inspector in 1727 and seems to have continued in the job until 1738 when he moved to Spotsylvania County. His brother, Dale Carter, succeeded him as Inspector. *William and Mary College Quarterly*, 28 (July 1909): 52.

[35]Stacy L. Lorenz, "'To Do Justice to His Majesty, The Merchant And The Planter': Governor William Gooch and the Virginia Tobacco Inspection Act of 1730," *Virginia Magazine of History and Biography*, 108(2000): 345-392.

[36]T.E. Campbell, *Colonial Caroline, A History of Caroline County, Virginia* (Richmond: The Dietz Press, 1954), 73. In fact, rioters burned several government tobacco warehouses in the Northern Neck in the winter of 1731-1732. Lorenz , 381.

[37]Edwin Conway to Lt. Gov. William Gooch, 9 October 1732. This letter is printed in Hayden, *Virginia Genealogies: Glassell*, 238-239. He cites C.P. 219.

[38]Lorenz, 380.

[39]Edwin Conway to Lt. Gov. William Gooch, 10 October 1732. Hayden, *Virginia Genealogies: Glassell*, 239.

[40]Lorenz, 387.

[41]Reprinted from the *Virginia Gazette*, Friday, April 15 to Friday, April 22, 1737 in Hayden, *Virginia Genealogies: Glassell*, 241-243.

[42] "A Boy's Retort," *William and Mary College Quarterly; Historical Magazine*, series 1, 11(July 1893): 265.

[43]Edwin Conway, letter to William Parks, *Virginia Gazette*, Friday, 17 November to Friday, 24 November 1738, reprinted in Hayden, *Virginia Genealogies: Glassell*, 242-243.

[44]Edwin Conway, gent. vs. Thomas Pinckard, gent. Lancaster County Court Order Book 9 (1743-1752): 64a.

[45]Edwin Conway to the editor, *Virginia Gazette*, 17 April 1752. Reprinted in *William and Mary College Quarterly; Historical Magazine*, series 1, 12 (April 1904): 212-214.

[46]Margaret H. Tupper, transcriber, *Vestry Book, 1739-1786. Christ Church Parish, Lancaster County, Virginia* (Irvington, Va: Foundation for Historic Christ Church, 1990), 12-13, 16-18. Vestry records are missing from 1754-1758 and again in 1761-1762, so that it is not possible to determine if Edwin Conway was still serving on the vestry. Vestrymen often, but not always, served until death.

[47]Lancaster County Court Order Book 11 (1756-1764): 195.

[48]"Excerpts from Journal of Col. James Gordon, of Lancaster County, Va." *William and Mary College Quarterly; Historical Magzine*, series 1, 11(1902-1903): 98-112.

[49]James Gordon diary entry, 17 July 1759, *William and Mary College Quarterly.*

[50]Ibid., 1 April 1763. *William and Mary Quarterly; Historical Magazine*, series 1, 12 (July, 1903): 4.

[51]21, 22 September, 4, 6 October 1763. Ibid., 9-10.

[52]Will of Col. Edwin Conway, 27 July 1762, probated 20 January 1764. Reprinted in Hayden, *Virginia Genealogies: Glassell*, 238-239.

Thomas Perkins, Mariner

Except for a lease agreement, an inventory, and a few other scattered documents, Thomas Perkins would have been a typical Christ Church parishioner whose name has been lost to history. He was not famous; he was not rich; he was not a criminal; he was, just like the majority of his fellow parishioners, average. The scattered clues to his life tell us about a time when water transportation was as important to the Tidewater colonists as was land travel.

Perkins' first appearance in the public records comes with his marriage on March 22, 1735, to Ellinor Currell. Both husband and wife were Christ Church parishioners, with Ellinor's family having resided there for several generations. Standing security for the marriage bond was Isaac Currell, who is not listed as Ellinor's father but was surely a kinsman, maybe a brother or more than likely her Uncle Isaac.[1] Although her parents remain somewhat of a mystery, a careful study of the records of her uncles creates the probability that her father was Jacob and her mother was Mary.[2]

Just like most people in the county, the Perkins family probably set up its household in a crude wooden structure, while raising a few crops and some livestock. Perkins' attention, however, appears to have been more focused on the water than on the land. In 1743 he leased 15 acres of land on a small creek with direct access to the Rappahannock River. The lease, from William Heard, was for 21 years beginning on December 25, 1743. The agreement cost Perkins £20 of "current money" immediately and then required that he pay an annual token fee of "one ear of Indian corn on Christmas Day" each year. The land, which was somewhere in the vicinity of Cherry Point, was just a small triangle off the Heard plantation, but it included "all the point of Land between the middle cove and the home creek."[3]

Perkins died in 1750, and an analysis of his inventory

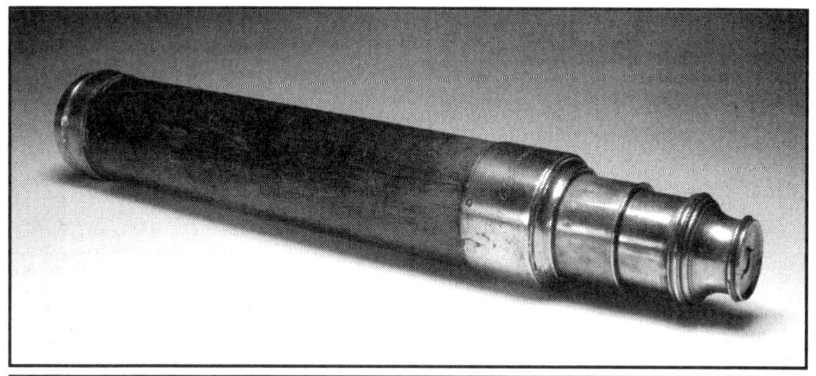

The "two spyglasses" in Perkins' estate inventory would have looked something like this mid-18th century telescope from the collection at the Mariners' Museum in Newport News. (Illustration courtesy the Mariners' Museum, Newport News)

shows that he certainly could not have been making much of a living from this farm. Seven head of cattle and two hoes are all he had to show for his agricultural efforts. On the other hand, he had a number of items that give some indication as to why he chose to rent a small piece of land with water access. One quarter of his inventory's value came from one item, a boat and rigging worth £30. Only his adult Negro slave, Sue, was valued higher at £33. He also owned "1 sea bed and hamack," "1 marriners cumpas," "2 spy glasses," "1 line and hooks," and "two sandglasses."[4]

Clearly the bit of wealth Perkins and his wife accumulated did not come from the land, but from the water. What else can be gleaned about Perkins from the public record? For one, he knew how to read, as his inventory contained half a dozen or so books, including two Bibles. Also, he had no qualms about engaging in the local legal system, for in 1745 he challenged George Jackson for killing his mare. The court found Jackson not guilty as charged, but at the end of the jury trial Perkins was awarded £4 in judgment.[5] Two years later, a gentleman named John Steptoe charged that Perkins owed him £1.19.5 on an account. When Perkins failed to appear in court, Steptoe was awarded the full amount plus costs.[6]

Without owning land, of course, Perkins could never aspire to the gentleman status that Steptoe enjoyed. Nonetheless, he had accumulated some nice possessions by the time he died in 1750. If his wealth came from the water, in what manner did he make his living? Did he transport goods for others, transport people, or engage in the trade of goods? He has one line and hooks, probably for fishing, but no fishing nets. Without those and possessing only a single line, he was probably not a fisherman by trade. The inclusion of rigging meant the boat had sails, but that is all we know. More than likely it was a small shallop, pinnace, or small schooner that roamed the Chesapeake Bay and the river mouths. However, the other seafaring items indicate that at times he must have roamed further to sea. The "sea bed and hamack" would have had no use on a pinnace because there was no place to hang the bedding. In addition, a knowledgeable mariner who kept to the bay waters would not have needed a mariner's compass. However, a sailor heading to the West Indies would probably have owned some tool to figure latitude as well, and there is no such tool in the inventory. Why does Perkins' inventory contain a pair of "poket stillards" and "a parcel of vials"? The stillards were miniature scales used to weigh something of value. Could he have been weighing Spanish coins – an important trade item of the period? What item of value would have been placed in the vials? Perhaps spices and dyes acquired from places like the West Indies, or perhaps just some common medicines of the time were in the vials. Was Perkins a sea captain for hire, meaning that he occasionally worked for the owners of larger ships, taking with him the necessary equipment such as a compass and seabed, and then returning to ply the waters of the bay in his own ship? Or perhaps his pinnace was one that was towed behind a merchant ship or even hoisted aboard for the journey down to Latin America. There is even the possibility that he was involved with smuggling, an apparently common occupation for the time period.[7]

In whatever manner he made his living, however, he managed to accumulate more than £120 worth of personal estate, including two slaves, and a boat and several pieces of precious metals. From his estate he chose to leave to his son, Thomas, a pair of gold buttons, a gold ring, and a pair of large silver buckles. Everything else went to his wife who administered his estate. Included in the household contents were two slaves, the woman named Sue and a boy named Jack who was valued at £12. Sue is probably the person appearing on the tithable list in 1746 when Perkins was taxed on himself and one Negro woman.[8] Inventory evidence for a more refined sense of living than one might expect to find from a small tenant farmer includes a looking glass, a watch, a nice bed, glass bottles, a copper kettle, and a bird in a cage.[9] The caged bird is particularly intriguing. Surely a local bird would not have been worthy of display in a cage. Perhaps the bird was more exotic – a parrot

Perkins' boat could very easily have looked like the shallops depicted in this 18th-century drawing. (Illustration courtesy the Mariners' Museum, Newport News)

from Central America for instance – of the type mariners some-times had.

What happened to the son Thomas is also a bit of a mystery. In 1771 "Captain" Thomas Perkins appears in the Lancaster marriage records as marrying Sarah Ann Currell whose father was G. Currell. If this Thomas Perkins was the son listed in the will, then he was marrying his cousin, a common occurrence for the time period. More interesting, however, is the title "captain." Was Thomas a captain in the militia or was he following in his father's footsteps and captaining a ship? The question remains unanswered.[10]

From the scanty bit of evidence we can learn much of Perkins as he went about life in Christ Church Parish. Here he was married, paid his taxes, wrested out a living from the waterways, had a child, quarreled a bit with his neighbors, and when he died he left a few tantalizing clues to make us wonder who he was.

ENDNOTES

[1]Lancaster County Marriage Register, 22 March 1735/36.

[2]Ellinor had a number of uncles who were apparently half brothers to each other, some being named Currell and some Martin. By the process of elimination, it appears that Jacob Currell, whose wife was Mary, had brothers Isaac and Abraham Currell and William Martin – all of whom were Ellinor's uncles. Jacob died in 1724, which is why Ellinor's Uncle Isaac might have been the witness and security for her marriage bond. In addition, George Currell served as one of the executors of Thomas Perkins' will. George was the grandson of Mary Harward, the mother of Mary Currell. Lancaster County Will Book 10:325, 332; Will Book 13:135; Will Book 16: 201, 231; Will Book 15:200; Lancaster marriage register.

[3]Lancaster County Deed and Will Book 14:4, Deed of Lease between William Heard and Thomas Perkins, recorded 13 January 1743.

[4]Lancaster County Deed and Will Book 14:308, Thomas Perkins inventory and appraisal, 14 September 1750.

[5]Lancaster County Court Order Book 9:77, 9 August 1745.

[6]Ibid., 9:138, 14 August 1747.

[7] Telephone interview, 30 January 2001, with research historian Josh Giml of the Mariners' Museum, Newport News.

[8]1746 Tithable list.

[9]Perkins inventory.

[10]Lancaster marriage register, p. 41, Captain Thomas Perkins to Sarah Ann Currell, 1771, consent given by G. Currell.

THE REVEREND JOHN BELL
CHRIST CHURCH PARISH RECTOR

In 1711, after the death of their popular minister Andrew Jackson, the vestry of Christ Church Parish sought a replacement. John Bell, the man they chose, remained more than three decades in the parish, a long tenure for a colonial Virginia clergyman, and became a well-established figure in the community.

His background is a mystery. Several writers have claimed that he was a graduate of Pembroke College, Oxford.[1] There is a possibility that he was not English, but a Scot, and may have graduated from one of the four universities in Scotland. His brother, Dr. Alexander Bell, who had a distinctly Scottish name, was also on the Northern Neck, and was one of several physicians who treated Robert "King" Carter. Christ Church Parish had been very pleased with its longtime Ulster Scots minister, Andrew Jackson, and had been served briefly by a French Huguenot prior to that. It would be no surprise to find the parish turning to another non-English minister, as it would do for Bell's successor, the Reverend David Currie, a Scot.

We do not know how the parish recruited Bell. His physician brother may already have been in the area and may have suggested his sibling's name to Robert Carter, vestryman and senior warden, who likely played an important role in the selection of the minister. On the other hand, Bell may have come to Christ Church Parish on recommendation from the governor, Alexander Spotswood, and the commissary, James Blair, who was the Bishop of London's representative in the colony and President of the College of William and Mary in Williamsburg.[2] Those officials liked to exercise what they considered their prerogative to recommend ministers for the Virginia parishes. However, at Christ Church, Lancaster, as in parishes across the colony, the vestry (the 12 laymen who governed the local church) was dominated by leading local planters who preferred to retain as much control over their parish affairs as possible, including the selection of the minister.[3]

We do know that Bell was ordained by the Bishop of London and on January 11, 1712, received the King's Bounty, a royal grant dispensed by the bishop for the purpose of paying the passage of clergymen serving in the British colonies. He was required to sail soon after and likely arrived in Virginia in the spring of 1712.[4] Bell probably paid his respects to the commissary in Williamsburg. Blair may have introduced him to Governor Spotswood as well, after which Bell traveled to Lancaster County to meet his vestry and settle into his glebe, the farm with a dwelling house that each parish was required by law to provide for its minister.

Bell came to Christ Church Parish and its partner, St. Mary's White Chapel Parish, at a time when the established church held the allegiance of nearly every Virginia resident. The church played an important role, not only as the center of the liturgical and moral life of the community, but as a focal point of its social life as well. All residents of the parish were required to attend the regular Sunday worship service at least once a month. From the time of his arrival, Bell preached at Christ Church once every Sunday and on Good Fridays, observing in a 1724 report to the Bishop of London that the "Church is thronged and almost all white persons in the parish (not necessarily hindered) attend. . . ." Bell was also responsible for conducting services at St. Mary's White Chapel. He preached there every other Sunday and on all special occasions. In his absence, the clerk read "the Common Prayer and an homily or sermon…." Three times a year, at Christmas, Easter, and Whitsunday (Pentecost), Bell administered the Holy Sacrament to 60 to 80 communicants.[5]

For his services, Bell reported that he earned 16,000 pounds "Aranoko" tobacco each year, a salary established by the House of Burgesses in 1696 and continued until the Revolution. Bell also received an allotment for the cask he needed to package his tobacco. Christ Church and St. Mary's shared the expenses, as each paid Bell 8,000 pounds and his cask allotment with funds raised by annual parish levies.[6] Bell had additional sources of income beyond the salary. It was customary in the Church of England for individual parishioners to pay the minister a fee for performing marriages, baptisms, funerals, and a service known as the churching of women, which took place after the birth of a child. These fees had been set in pounds of tobacco by the colony's General Assembly in 1631: 20 for a marriage service, and 10 each for churchings and burials.[7] Bell also received payment for providing sermons for neighboring parishes in need of a minister. In October of 1723, for example, the vestry of St. Stephen's Parish in nearby Northumberland County paid Bell 450 pounds of tobacco for each of the eight sermons he delivered. He preached 35 sermons for 400 pounds tobacco each for neighboring Wicomico Parish from 1723 to 1727.[8] In addition, Bell farmed the glebe lands (which totalled 839 acres), where he could raise food for his family and servants and produce a tobacco crop for the market.

Although the vestry book that contained details of the early operation of Christ Church Parish disappeared more than a century ago,[9] Bell's 1724 report to the Bishop of London provides important insight into the parish and its minister. From this report we know that after 12 years' residency, Bell had not been inducted into the parish, a status that would have guaranteed him life tenure as rector. He must, therefore, have been kept on an annual contract, indicating the power of the vestry. Whether he was ever subsequently inducted we do not know, but it is unlikely.

Bell estimated that there were 300 families in his combined Christ Church-St. Mary's White Chapel Parish. In addition, there were "a great many Black bond men and women infidels that understand not our Language nor me their's: not any free." In spite of the cultural, racial, and linguistic barrier, Bell indicated that "the Church is open to them; the word preached, and the Sacraments administered with circumspection."

Bell noted that there was no public school in the parish,

nor any parochial library. However, he indicated that he provided instruction in the catechism for the parish youth during Lent. He regretted that parents, masters, and mistresses were lax in seeing that the young people were brought to the church for that purpose. Otherwise, he offered no complaint about the operation of the parish. His house was kept in good repair at the expense of both parishes, and the church was provided with everything required for the proper conduct of worship services except a surplice for Bell. Virginia law required the surplice, a white linen garment with flowing sleeves, gathered at the yoke, and worn over the black ministerial gown, be worn by Church of England clergy. Other protestant ministers, especially Presbyterians, did not wear a surplice. The failure of the Christ Church vestry to provide a surplice could reflect its members' long experience with non-Anglican ministers and their belief that this vestment was not necessary.[10]

It is curious that Bell's report stated that the parish had no library. The Reverend Andrew Jackson had specified in his will that his own library be left to the parish for the use of the incumbent. John Bell's estate inventory, taken in February 1744, showed a significant personal library. It is possible that many of these books had belonged to Jackson. Unfortunately, those who took the inventory grouped the books in units such as "4 divine books," 4 latten books" or "13 large old books." This makes it difficult to know just what authors and titles were represented. In some cases, however, these are indicated, giving a notion of his theological interests. Bell had a *History of the Reformation of the Church of England*, a commentary on the Book of Revelation, *The History of the Jews and Neighboring Nations*, and sets of sermon volumes by South,

Stanhope, Black, and Bradley. He had a large Bible in old print (Gothic type) and a new Bible, several English dictionaries, Mercer's *Abridgement*, a concordance, and *The Whole Duty of Man*, one of the most popular devotional works among Anglicans. Non-religious works included two law books, many "latten" (Latin) books, and an Aesop's Fables.[11]

Bell may have been married when he arrived in Virginia. Robert Carter recorded in his diary that on Saturday, November 21, 1724, "Mrs. Bell died."[12] By January 1728, Bell had married Elizabeth Jones (1707-1749), for Carter recorded that on January 2, 1728, "Mr. Bell & his wife came here" (to Corotoman).[13] She was the daughter of Captain William Jones, Jr., of Hickory Neck, Northumberland County and his wife Leanna Lee, daughter of Captain Charles Lee of Cobbs Hall, Northumberland County.[14] John Bell was the father of nine children, five sons and four daughters, most, if not all of them by his (second) wife, Elizabeth Jones Bell. The sons were William, Thomas, James, John, and Charles. The daughters were Ann, who married her cousin, Captain William Jones; Margaret, wife of Shapleigh Neale; Elizabeth, and Mary, whose married name was Burnley.[15]

Bell acquired considerable Virginia land during his long service in Lancaster County. His first acquisition occurred in 1719, when he purchased two tracts totaling 395 acres on "Corotoman Neck."[16] Next, he acquired substantial acreage, 2,470 acres, in Prince William County, perhaps from Robert Carter when he was still agent for Lord Fairfax. Bell's brother, Dr. Alexander Bell, had left land in Prince William County to three of Bell's children: 1,110 acres to daughter Margaret, and an unspecified amount (probably 1,200 acres) to sons William and Thomas. In addition, Bell had a house and lot in Falmouth town, a shipping port in King George County opposite present Fredericksburg.[17]

Bell prospered sufficiently to provide a respectable cash dowry for each of his daughters. His will indicated that he gave £200 each for daughters Margaret and Elizabeth. Mention of a

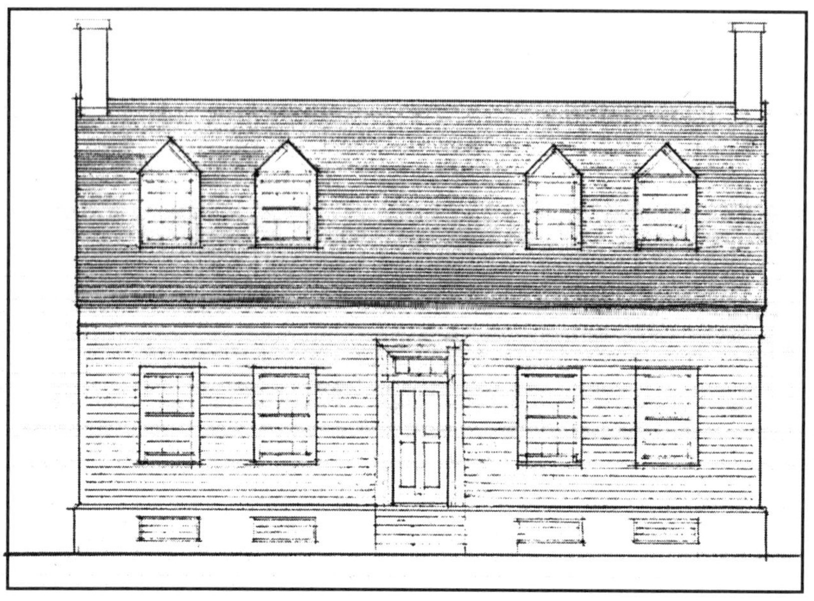

This conjectural drawing of the Christ Church Glebe House, which was provided to Bell by the vestry, is based upon information in the vestry minutes concerning a potential modernization of the dwelling in 1743. (Drawing by Dickson McKenna)

balance bequeathed to his grandson, Charles Jones, due from the dowry of the child's deceased mother, Ann Bell Jones, suggests that Bell allocated her that amount also.[18]

No journal, diary, account book, or letter from John Bell is known to have survived. Most of what we know of this decent, faithful clergyman must be wrung from his report to the bishop, land records, his will, and his estate inventory. There are a few glimpses of the lighter side of the parish parson in the diary of his most powerful parishioner, Robert Carter. There we learn that Bell came to Corotoman from time to time on social visits, and that Carter also visited socially in Bell's home at the glebe. In January 1728, Carter recorded that "Mr. Bell & his wife came here. I sat up till almost 12 at play, lost 7 bits," indicating a relationship that was close enough to share simple gaming pleasures and strong enough to survive minor gambling losses of the rich man to the parson. Bell, for his part, was confident enough in the relationship that he could offer public criticism from the pulpit of Carter and court clerk, Thomas Edwards, when the two powerful men were feuding.[19]

Bell may have been privy to Robert Carter's thinking about and planning for a new church for his parish. We can only guess at this, for no evidence survives in vestry books or private papers. It is certain, however, that Bell was the last minister to serve the wooden church that Robert Carter's father, John Carter, built in 1669 and that John Carter II completed in 1670. Bell was the first minister to serve in the magnificent new church that Robert Carter planned and donated but did not see to completion. The church's benefactor remembered his minister in his will, leaving him £10 for mourning. Bell may also have been one of the 30 friends and relatives to receive a gold mourning ring.[20]

Bell was an excellent example of the close relationship that developed between the powerful planter gentry and the clergy of the established church in colonial Virginia. Although we do not know if Bell came from a gentry family originally, it is clear that he was living the life of a comfortable gentleman planter in Lancaster County. At the time of his death in 1743, he owned nearly 3,000 acres in three counties, 85 head of livestock and 3 horses in Lancaster and 57 head of livestock in Prince William. His slaveholdings consisted of 26 slaves (15 men or boys and 11 women or girls) in Lancaster and 17 slaves (11 male, 6 female) in Prince William. Few men in Christ Church Parish could match that wealth.

The Bell family lived in comfort but not luxury at the glebe. Furniture at the house included four bedsteads and bedding, a trundle bed, 16 leather-covered chairs, a corner cupboard, a desk, four tables, three trunks, eight chests, three looking glasses. A mixture of earthenware and pewter served for dishes. Luxury items included a large silver tankard from which Bell no doubt took his cider and beer, silver teaspoons and other spoons, silver salt cellars and tongs, silver shoe and knee buckles, and a silver pocket watch.

Bell's 27 head of sheep, 32 pounds of unspun wool, and two spinning wheels indicated serious wool production on the glebe. There were no sheep on his Prince William land but some 21 head of cattle and 34 hogs and pigs, indicating meat production for family, servants, and possibly for the market. His tobacco stores at the time of his death consisted of 4,000 pounds in Prince William and 17,140 pounds in Lancaster. Because his widow would have to vacate the glebe house at his death so that it could be turned over to the new minister, Bell provided that the proceeds from the sale of tobacco from the glebe and the Prince William plantation, as well as the levy from the two parishes, be allocated to build a house on his land at Corotoman Neck for his wife's home during the remainder of her life. At her death, that land would go to their son Charles.[21]

Social historians have suggested in recent years that it was the lifestyle, the accumulation of wealth, the association with the gentry, the participation in card-playing, and minor gaming that led many Virginians to turn away from the Anglican clergy as their spiritual leaders. Within a few years of Bell's death, evangelical preachers appeared in Virginia offering a somber lifestyle, plainer living, and a more vibrant, experiential brand of religious expression. Emboldened to criticize the established church clergy, some of these men found in their congregations an eager and sympathetic audience. Lancaster County became the scene of such preaching. Bell, who represented the best of the older style clergy who served the established church in Virginia at the peak of its power and influence, did not live to experience that loss of respect and influence. He surely climbed the steps in pride mixed with humility to the grand pulpit of the new Christ Church to address his flock, rich and poor, black and white, gathered in the fine paneled pews below.[22]

ENDNOTES

[1]Joan R. Gunderson, *The Anglican Ministry in Virginia, 1723-1766: A Study of a Social Class* (New York & London: Garland Publishing Co., 1989) and Joseph Venn *Alumni Oxoniensis.* The Rev. Dr. G. McLaren Brydon, longtime historiographer of the Diocese of Virginia, stated that there is no record of Bell's

graduation from Oxford or Cambridge and suggested the possibility of a Scottish university. Brydon to Marie Bell Ellis, 2 April 1938.

[2] A good discussion of the role of the commissary is found in Robert W. Prichard, *A History of the Episcopal Church* (Harrisburg, Pa.: Morehouse Publishing, 1991), 27-30. Blair, who served as commissary from 1689 to 1743, was a powerful figure in colonial Virginia who succeeded in having two royal governors removed.

[3] The strong vestry system did not exist in England. It is a development of the colonial Virginia established church and became an integral part of its successor denomination, the Episcopal Church. For a good discussion of this laicization of the church see John Frederick Woolverton, *Colonial Anglicanism in North America,* (Detroit: Wayne State University Press 1984), 74-80.

[4] Some sources indicate Bell came to the parish in 1711. His receipt of the King's Bounty payment of £20 for the transatlantic voyage occurred in January 1711/12. This required him to sail within a month. Because at that time the new year did not begin until 25 March, January dates were reported as 1711 or as 1711/12. The length of a typical transatlantic voyage that began in late January or early February would generally mean arrival in Virginia in April, by which time the calendar dates would all be 1712.

[5] John Bell, 1724 Report to the Bishop of London. See *Christ Church, Lancaster County, Virginia* (Irvington, Va.: Foundation for Historic Christ Church, 2001), Appendix II. At Easter services on 10 April 1726, parishioner Robert Carter noted that "Mr. Bell preachd an excellent sermon. The greatest number of communicants that ever I saw." Robert Carter Diary 1722-1728, 25 September 1722. Transcribed from a partially corrected, typed transcript property of the University of Virginia Library, lent by Francis L. Berkeley, solely for reference and research use by the Historic Christ Church Foundation volunteers. Although the number of communicants seems low by standards of the year 2002, for a parish of 300 families, it was typical of Anglican churches in Maryland, Virginia, and South Carolina in that same 1724 Report and greater than that reported in the English Diocese of Oxford. Prichard, *A History of the Episcopal Church*, 38-39.

[6] William Waller Hening, ed., *The Statutes at Large; Being a Collection of All the Laws of Virginia,* III, 152. In his report to the bishop, Bell indicated his income was 16,000 pounds of Aranoko tobacco, probably including the allotment for cask. He indicated that the fee was levied on 1,100 tithables, and that its value in sterling was £80 per year. In colonial Virginia, there were two varieties of tobacco that were grown: sweetscented and Oronoco, the first being more valuable than the second. Bell was paid in the lesser grade of tobacco.

[7] Hening, *Statutes,* I (1631): 160.

[8] Vestry book of St. Stephen's Parish, Northumberland, quoted in William Meade, *Old Churches, Ministers, and Families of Virginia,* Vol. II (reprint, Baltimore: Genealogical Publishing Company, 1966), 467 and John L. Overholt and Arthur C. Johnson, *The History of Wicomico Parish, including 1703-1795 Vestry Minutes* (Wicomico Parish Church, Va., 1998), 32-33, 36-37, 44, 72-73.

[9] There are no routine vestry business records surviving for Christ Church Parish until 1759. The vestry book beginning in 1739 that Margaret Tupper has transcribed is, until 1759, principally a vestry book for St. Mary's White Chapel Parish, but it contains the general vestry meeting minutes for the combined parishes of Christ Church and St. Mary's White Chapel. Be-

cause the two parishes shared a minister and a glebe, their two vestries met in a combined general vestry to deal with matters pertaining to the minister and the glebe property. In 1752 the two parishes were combined by order of the Virginia legislature.

[10]John Bell, 1724 Report to the Bishop of London.

[11]Inventory of the Reverend John Bell, 12 February 1744. Lancaster County Will Book 14:46. Those who made the inventory were Nicholas Martin, Epaphroditus Lawson, Ezekiel Gilbert, Abraham Currell, and the widow, Elizabeth Bell.

[12]Robert Carter Diary 1722-1728, 21 November 1724. Transcribed from a partially corrected, typed transcript property of the University of Virginia Library, lent by Francis L. Berkeley, solely for reference and research use by the Historic Christ Church Foundation volunteers. It is also possible that this was not the wife of the Reverend John Bell but rather of Dr. Alexander Bell.

[13]Ibid., 2 January 1727/28.

[14]Leanna Lee was a granddaughter of Richard Lee, progenitor of the prominent Lee family of the Northern Neck, and his wife, Ann Constable. See John Bell research file at Historic Christ Church Foundation for various genealogical materials relating to Bell's in-laws in the Lee and Jones families.

[15]Published tales of a daughter who came from England with Bell, and who died and was buried by her request at the glebe, then removed by her clergyman-father to the church cemetery, for which she appeared as a ghost to her father until he returned her remains to the glebe have no substantiation in any contemporary documentation. Marguerite du Pont Lee, *Virginia Ghosts* (Berryville, Va.: Virginia Book Company, 1966, revised edition), 48; Marie Bell Ellis, "Bell and Allied Families," unpublished manuscript, Los Gatos, Calif, 1968; and John Bell will, 10 June 1743, Lancaster County Will Book 13:334.

[16]The first tract, 80 acres, was purchased from William Olivet, and the larger one, 315 acres, from Damerson Pasquet. William Olivet to John Bell, 9 February 1719, Lancaster County Deed Book 11:145; Damerson Pasquet to John Bell, 9 February 1719, Lancaster Deed Book 11:147.

[17]Will of the Reverend John Bell, written 6 January 1742, proved 10 June 1743. Lancaster County Will Book 13:334.

[18]Ibid.

[19]Robert Carter Diary 1722-1728, 25 December 1722, 30 July 1723, 14 September 1723, 2 January 1727/28. Transcribed from a partially corrected, typed transcript property of the University of Virginia Library, lent by Francis L. Berkeley, solely for reference and research use by the Historic Christ Church Foundation volunteers.

[20]Robert Carter will, page 32. Typed transcript, FHCCRF. Carter specified that the money was to provide a mourning [suit] for the minister. Carter left the same amount to his son-in-law, Dr. George Nicholas, for a mourning suit, but sums of £20 each to sons-in-law Page and Harrison to purchase their mourning suits.

[21]John Bell will. Mrs. Bell's house is sketched on a map of the Corrotoman River made in 1790, a copy in FHCCRF. It was located on a point at the mouth of Zeek's Creek, which is now known as Bell's Creek.

[22]This biographical sketch is an expansion of one prepared by FHCC staff for use in docent training for the visitors and the school programs.

Mary Landon Jones Swan
Gentlewoman

On February 22, 1670, in St. Martins in the Fields, Middlesex, England, Thomas and Mary Landon presented their first daughter to be baptized as Mary. On May 10, 1683, at Credenhill, the Landon estate in Herefordshire, Mary, her brothers, and sister, Anne, witnessed the baptism of the last daughter to be born to the family. She was named Elizabeth and affectionately called "Betty."[1]

The Landon children were raised in privileged circumstances. Credenhill, the manor house that was the family home in southwest central England, was an ancient hereditary site.[2] Here on the beautiful lawns and in the gardens, the children could run and play and stretch their imaginations as they explored the crumbling Roman ruins nearby.[3] Their father, Thomas, was an officer in the Royal Court of Charles II, where he held the position of Gentleman Groom of the King's Buttery.[4] He probably retained that position into the reign of James II, King Charles' successor, but it is possible that he lost that office during the Glorious Revolution of 1688.[5] Mary, by then married to John Jones, and the mother of two sons, still had close ties with her family and especially with her youngest sister, Betty.[6]

In 1693 or 1694, Thomas and Mary Landon and several of their children, including St. Leger, Roger, Betty, Mary, and her husband, John Jones, immigrated to Virginia. Before the family left England, Thomas Landon contracted with three men to serve him in varying capacities when they settled in the colony. They too accompanied the family on the voyage.[7] Mary and John's two boys apparently remained in England, most likely still in school and in the care of Mary's brother, Silvanus, and sister, Anne. Silvanus became President of the English company at Baudjarmassingh in India. Anne was married first to William Ryfort of London and then to the Reverend Thomas Wheatland.

Another brother who remained behind, the Reverend John Landon, served at Madras Patnam.[8]

Apparently the Landons accommodated quickly to their new Virginia environs. Thomas Landon acquired considerable land in Middlesex County and was appointed justice of the county court. Betty married Richard Willis, a wealthy landowner in the county.[9] When Thomas Landon returned to England on business in 1697, he gave his two sons-in-law, John Jones and Captain Richard Willis, power of attorney in his absence.[10] Just four years later, in 1700, Thomas Landon was dead and both Mary and Betty were widowed.[11]

John Jones probably died around April 1700, for Mary Jones is named on a bond to administer his estate on May 6, 1700.[12] In November 1700, Thomas Landon wrote his will, which was probated three months later on February 3, 1701. He left most of his estate to his wife, but he provided "to Capt. Richard Willis my son-in-law & his wife Betty Willis and likewise to my Daughter Mary Jones three rings of Gold of fiveteen shillings Price each to be Delivered as soon as Conveniently they may be had from England."[13]

About that same time, Richard Willis died, leaving Betty a wealthy widow. By April 1701, the attractive young widow, Betty Landon Willis, was betrothed to Col. Robert Carter of Corotoman in Lancaster County. As an assurance of a suitable dower for Betty, should he predecease her, Carter deeded 180 acres of land, part of his Corotoman estate, to William Armistead, William Ball, and Mary Landon Jones on Betty's behalf. In conjunction with this conveyance, Mary appointed Alexander Swan as her attorney (representative).[14]

Alexander Swan, a captain in the militia, had served two terms in the House of Burgesses in the 1690s alongside Robert Carter, and had also been High Sheriff of Lancaster County. He may have been an attorney, for he represented Robert Carter often in business dealings and legal matters.[15]

Swan, also recently widowed from his second wife, Elizabeth, courted Mary and took her as his third wife. His daugh-

Mary Swan's sister, Betty, married Robert "King" Carter, the most powerful man in Lancaster County. (Photo courtesy Shirley Plantation)

ters were married, but his young son John was still living at home on the easternmost 200 acres on Fleets Bay Neck, a tract that Swan just purchased in 1700.[16] Capt. Alexander Swan was a man of means, so Mary's position in a prestigious family and as sister-in-law to the most powerful and wealthy man in the area seemed a continuum of her life of privilege and comparative ease. She assumed the role easily as mistress of a large plantation, overseeing the many responsibilities of the domestic side of their lives. To add to her contentment, with her own sons so far away, she doted on her young sister's growing family.[17]

Alexander Swan died in 1709. His will stipulated that his estate remain intact and the profits be divided between his son and heir John, son of Swan's first wife Judith Hinds, and his widow, Mary Landon Jones Swan. The will although carefully conceived, created an enmity that would persist for 20 years. Son John was heir to the estate, but if he died without issue, his sisters Margaret Pinckard and Judith Jones would inherit the property. Mary's life estate was contingent upon the proviso that ". . . if wife Mary go to England to get her share of her brother Sylvanus' estate and does not agree that his [Swan's] children share in her inheritance, Mary is no longer to share in profits of the estate." He named Brother Robert Carter and wife, Mary, as Executors of his will.[18]

It does not appear that Mary returned to England, nor do the records reveal the circumstances under which Mary and her stepson John Swan lived for the next few years. John married Sarah Ingram about 1716. The young couple soon had two little girls, Judith and Ann.[19] One would expect that it was a reasonably happy time. Mary's well-being and comfort seemed assured. That was not to be. Instead, records indicate that Mary's last years were fraught with anxiety, abuse, and discord. The most crushing blow was the loss of her beloved sister Betty, who died shortly after the birth of her 10th child, George.

There were undoubtedly problems from the onset between John Swan and his father's widow, each resenting having to share what they thought was rightfully theirs. Dissension grew and the situation became untenable. With Robert Carter as co-complainant, Mary filed suit against John Swan.

> 1720 11 May
> In the difference . . . between Mary Swan, Extx of the last will and testament of Alexander Swan and John Swan, defendant . . . for his hindering the Complainant from enjoying any part of the Testator's estate or

haveing any part in the Execon of the Last Will and Testament of the sd. Alexander Swan or suffering the profits of the aforesaid . . . and allsoe for assigning to himself the whole power of the estate . . . and allsoe for his the defendants keeping stocks of cattle sheep hoggs and horses and workeing his own slaves on the plantacion whereon the aforesd testator lived . . . to the destruction and impoverishing of testated . . . and allsoe for the defendants abuseing the Complt and destroying what she had on the plantacon. . . . the court here haveing viewed the plantacon whereon the aforesd testator lived and dyed ether with the dwelling house and other dwellings thereon allsoe the slaves and the stock of cattle . . . and truly informed themselves of the several other tracts of lands and plantacons belonging to the aforesd testator . . . to enable themselves to make an Equitable decree . . . and haveing heard allsoe the severall allegacons & proofs as well [on both sides] . . . it appears to this Court that the aforesd John Swan . . . by assumeing to himself the sole management of power . . . contrary to the will of Alexander Swan it is impossible that the sd will should be fulfilled and kept . . . or that the Complt and defendt should ever peaceably cohabit & abide upon one and the same plantacon. . . . [20]

The Court decreed that Mary was to be fully compensated for her losses with an equitable division of the estate, but she gave up the home she had known for nearly a decade. Mary spent the rest of her life at Corotoman in the home of Robert Carter.[21] Now her only comfort was in the staunch support of her brother-in-law and the company of her beloved nieces and nephews.

John Swan died in the summer of 1721 at the age of 29, but there was no peace for Mary.[22] The grief and turmoil of her late years had taken its toll and her life was nearing its end. John Bell, the minister of Christ Church was summoned.

1721 21 January
Sunday evening 9 a Clock
Attending on Mrs Mary Swan she being sound in
memory and judgment but low and weak in body according to my office, about 4 a Clock this after-noon, I
counseled her to get in order her worldly business,
that she might not have anything of that nature to dis-
turb her in her last moments, her answer to me was in
the form as far as I can remember, I leave the arrange-
ments to my brother, meaning as I understood her,
Robert Carter Esq. I told her it was fit then to commit
it in writing, her answer was yes., yes accordingly Mr
Turberville . . . pen ink and paper being ready I went
to wait upon her and after having signified that we
were come to do her that service the confirming will...
replyed to me she was quite weary and tired out and
inclined therefor to take rest. Between eight and nine
I went to visit her again and found her so near the
pangs of death that I thought fit to read over the agony
prayer.
Written and signed this Jan evening at ten a Clock
John Bell [letters following name indecipherable] [23]

On her last day on earth, Mary was able to converse with
an intimate, whose deposition regarding the conversation was
recorded as Mary's nuncupative will.

1721 21 January
The will of Mary Swan declared unto Isabel Clements
the day and year above written. Vizt: The sd Isabel
asking of her whether she would not make a will and
settle her affairs, she answered it would be well if it
were done. Then the sd Isabel asked her how she
would dispose of her negroes. She said she would give
Tom to Lucie Carter and her girl Lyda to her oldest
son, Landon. Then the sd Isabel told her she had gold
rings and asked her how many she had, she replied
she had six here and one coming in. Then the sd Isabel
asked her who she would give her rings too, she answered she would give her wedding rings to her two

sons, then the sd Isabel told her she had a diamond ring and who would she give that too, she answered to Mary Carter then Isabel asked her if she had no friend here to give anything to, she answered friend, No — 'but she desired Judith Steptoe might have a ring. [There follows many bequests of household goods to Robert Carter's daughters, her nieces]. . . . then Isabel said you have given all to the three maidens [Ann, Mary and Lucie Carter] and have forgot Mr. George. [Robert Carter's youngest son] she answered no, no I will not forget George Carter . . . then Isabel said unto her can't you think of no honest person to administer on your estate she answered, my brother [Robert Carter] have had the trouble of it all along and it was her desire that he and Ann Carter should administer upon it.
Signed, Isabel Clements[24]

In February 1722, Robert Carter was appointed Administrator of the estate of Mary Swan. Seven months later he submitted an account of his administration.[25] On August 4, 1722, Sarah Swan, John's widow, married Thomas Edwards, the clerk of Lancaster County.[26] A year later, Edwards, on his wife's behalf, lodged an objection in court regarding the funeral expenses for Mary Swan as charged in Carter's accounting of her estate.[27]

In correspondence in July 1723 with Mary's son, Landon, regarding her estate, Robert Carter's disdain for the principals involved is made abundantly clear.

Rappahannock, Virginia
Mr. Landon Jones, London, England
. . . relating to the Death of your mother and her circumstances, I now send you an answer to. You already know she was at Law most of her widdowhood with her son-in-law [stepson] Swan . . . a most Virulent and Venemous person he was. He married the daughter of one Ingram who had

the reputaton of the most Litigious Hypocritical Knave there was in the County where he lived. Between them both your mother was baited like a bear at a stake the uneasiness and disturbance they gave her, she often said would hasten her to her grave. Her son Swan died some months before her and Ingram within a week after her. These three litigants going off so near one another, I little expected any new trouble would arise about this little triffle of an estate, but Swan's widow hath married with one Thomas Edwards, a little petty Fogging lawyer, the Clerk of our County, that hath as much mettle and more cunning for contention than his predecessor had and hath commenced against me as your mother's administrator two suits to our last Generall Court the one in chancery and the other in debt for 40 Pds. sterling . . . your mother and Swan entered into Articles of Accomodation. He was to make several buildings for her Residence to deliver up half her husband's estate lands etc. the profits whereof she was to enjoy during her life . . . nothing was done towards these buildings . . . and yet this Edwards thinks it a great piece of Justice to contend for this money.
Yr. Affectionate Kinsman & Humble Servt
Robert Carter, Esq.[28]

In a letter dated June 26, 1729, Carter informed Landon Jones that the courts had not yet settled the case with Edwards. He further indicated that little could come of it, for "she was more in debt than what her estate was valued to."[29] Controversy seemed to pursue this English-born gentlewoman to her Virginia grave and beyond, even when she was but a memory.

ENDNOTES

[1]"Account of the Family of Monnington and Credenhill, County Hereford: 1912 Tabular Pedigree of the Landon Family" included with a letter from Lloyd T. Smith, Jr., to Mrs. Walter Rogers, Foundation for Historic Christ Church, 15 February 1994. FHCCRF - Landon folder.

[2]Credenhill appears as Grednal on the gravestone of Betty Landon Carter at Christ Church. This spelling is likely a clue to the pronunciation of the name of the estate.

[3]Lloyd T. Smith, Jr., to Mrs. Walter Rogers, 15 February 1994. FHCCRF - Landon folder.

[4]"The Landon Family," *Virginia Magazine of History and Biography* (hereafter *VMHB*), 2(1894-5): 431-433. A groom was one of several officers in the household of a British sovereign. Buttery in this British usage comes from the Old French *boterie* (cask) and refers to a pantry or wine cellar. William Morris, ed., *American Heritage Dictionary of the English Language* (New York: Houghton Mifflin, 1973).

[5]Sources have not been located that offer specific information about the political affiliation of Thomas Landon. That as a supporter and retainer of the Stuarts, Charles II and James II, he lost his post in the accession of William and Mary to the throne in 1688 is certainly a possibility.

[6]"Landon Family," *VMHB*, 2 (1894-5): 432

[7]"Council Proceedings," *VMHB* 4 (1896-1897): 365n quotes from a deposition, probably from Middlesex County records, of Thomas Powell, formerly of the City of Hereford, stating that about January 1693/94, he was present when Henry Nixon made a contract with Mr. Thomas Landon to come to Virginia and serve him for two years, being paid 50 shillings the last year. A deposition of the same Thomas Powell, March 4, 1694, that he was present at a contract (made some time before we came from Hereford about the end of Dec. 1693) between Mr. Thomas Landon and Luke Matthews of the City of Hereford by which the latter agreed to serve Mr. Landon for two years as a tailor at 6d. a day. Articles of Agreement found in Middlesex County Deed Book 2: 115-116 dated 11 May 1696 refer to an agreement between Thomas Landon and Luke Mathews, tailor, made December 20, 1693, for service to Landon for two years and mention specifically that Thomas Landon planned to emigrate on a ship called *Bagnalls* bound for the Carolinas. Nell Marion Nugent, *Cavaliers and Pioneers, III, 1695-1732* (Richmond: Virginia State Library, 1979), [Patent Book 9], 93 [Land grants for headrights] John Hay and Christopher Robinson for transportation of 66 persons [including] . . . Thomas Landon, John Jones, Mary Jones, Roger Landon, Thomas Powell, Luke Matthews, Henry Nixon, Selenger [misreading of St. Leger] Landon, Thomas Landon, Mary Landon, Betty Landon. . . . [The only Jones family members listed are John and Mary, indicating that the two sons mentioned in Mary's will remained in England.]

[8]"Account of the Family of Monnington and Credenhill." See also Charles P. Keith, "The Landon Family," *VMHB*, 2 (1895): 430-433 for information about the will of Silvanus Landon, written at Batavia on 1 December 1704, probated 13 July 1708 in England. The Madras branch of the Landon family is said to have continued there until c. 1800.

[9]"Council Proceedings," *VMHB* 4 (1896-1897): 365.

43

[10]Power of attorney from Thomas Landon to Capt. Richd Willis and Mr. John Jones, 27 March 1697. Middlesex County Deed Book 2:175.

[11]Keith, "The Landon Family," *VMHB*, 5: 430-433.

[12]Bond for administration of the estate of John Jones. Middlesex County Deed Book 2:349-350.

[13]The fact that John Jones is named with Richard Willis in a 1696 deed, but not in a 1699 deed, and that Richard Willis is named in Thomas Landon's 1700 will but that John Jones is not would be strong indication of a death date between 1697 and 1699 for Jones. Thomas Landon Will, Middlesex County Will Book A: 139. The will, written in November 1700, was probated in February 1701.

[14]"Tithables of Lancaster County, Va., 1654," *VMHB* 5 (1898): 251; Ruth and Sam Sparacio, eds., *Deed and Will Abstracts of Lancaster County, Virginia, 1661-1702* (McLean, Va.: The Antient Press, 1991), 106-107.

[15]Christine Adams Jones, compiler, *Order Book Entries at Lancaster County Courthouse Referring to "Robert Carter of Corotoman" 1663-1731* (FHCCRF), 17 April 1699, Lancaster County Order Book 3: 158; *VMHB* 15: 442.

[16]Christ Church Parish, Lancaster County, Virginia, Rent Rolls 1720-1750, copies in FHCCRF, used with permission of The Huntington Library, San Marino, California; Christ Church Parish Processioners returns, 1711-1783.

[17]Betty Landon Carter bore Robert Carter 10 children.

[18]Will of Alexander Swan, 18 March 1709, probated 10 May 1710. Lancaster County Will Book 10:11. Alexander Swan's first wife had been Judith Hinds, whom he married on 15 November 1678. *Virginia Magazine of History and Biography*, 3 (1895-1896): 124.

[19]Ruby Lee Edwards, *Doctor Richard Edwards: Some of His Descendants and Allied Families*, (self-published, undated), Mary Ball Washington Museum and Library, Lancaster, Virginia.

[20]See entry for 11 May 1720 in Christine Adams Jones, compiler, "Order Book Entries at Lancaster County Court House, Lancaster, Virginia, referring to Robert Carter of 'Corotoman,' (1663-1732)," at FHCCRF.

[21]In a letter from Robert Carter to Mary's son Landon Jones in England, written on 22 July 1723, Carter noted, "She lived and died with me, for some years before her death. . . ."

[22]John Swan inventory. 11 April 1722. Lancaster County Will Book 10:335

[23]Lancaster County Will Book 10:363.

[24]Ibid.

[25]Jones, "Order Book Entries. . . Robert Carter," Lancaster County Court Order Book 7:26, 118.

[26]Lancaster County Marriage Register, Lancaster County Court House.

[27]Lancaster County Court Order Book 7:118.

[28]Robert Carter Letterbook #1, 63-65 (transcriptions of letterbook in possession of University of Virginia).

[29]Robert Carter Letterbook #6, 77

Robert Biscoe,
Indentured Bookkeeper
Published Author

In a poor London neighborhood, far from the pastoral Hampton Court Palace where King William III preferred to live, Elizabeth, wife of fishmonger John Biscoe, bore a son on November 27, 1699. The birth may have occurred above a shop Biscoe ran, where the strong odor of fish assailed the nose night and day. The couple named their boy Robert, perhaps for a grandfather, and may have had him baptized at Holy Trinity Parish Church.[1]

At the time Robert Biscoe was born, Robert Carter, a prominent planter in Christ Church Parish, Lancaster County, Virginia, was grieving the death of his wife and worrying over the care of his motherless children.[2] The London fishmonger and his wife could not have guessed that such a man as Carter would lift their young son from his simple circumstances in the mean streets and offer him a new life in Virginia.

John Biscoe probably died when his son was young, leaving an impoverished widow to support the boy, and possibly other children. Perhaps the rector of Holy Trinity saw a good mind in the lad and arranged for him to receive a remarkable education available only to poor boys and girls. In 1709, at the age of 10, Robert Biscoe was admitted to one of England's great public schools, Christ's Hospital.[3]

Edward VI had chartered Christ's Hospital as a school for poor children on property his father had seized from monks. Scholars who entered at age 10 or 11 emerged several years later well trained in reading, in writing a clear, distinguishable script known for centuries as "Christ's Hospital hand," and in basic double-entry bookkeeping.[4] As a scholar, Biscoe wore knee breeches and the long blue coat with silver buttons and leather belt for which Christ's Hospital was dubbed the "Bluecoat School."

The "Blues," as the graduates were known, were much in demand in the American colonies. School governors included the architect Christopher Wren and the physicist Isaac Newton, who helped establish there the Royal Mathematical School to provide navigators for the Royal Navy and merchant marine. This strengthened the school's colonial ties. The students received an education equivalent to that of the gentry and aristocracy at Eton and Harrow. While trained in the practical arts, they were also versed in music, drawing, and Latin.

Shipmasters and merchants in the thirteen colonies sent back to London to obtain a Blue as an apprentice.[5] A prominent Virginia planter, William Fitzhugh, wrote to a London merchant in 1690 that his brother promised to get him "an ingenious boy out of the Hospital who can write read & cast accounts." William Byrd, another great planter, had taken two Blues through his London agent. From such sources Robert Carter knew the reputation of Blues.[6]

In 1713, Carter took a 14-year-old Blue, John Parry, through his London agent, the merchant Micajah Perry, who also served Byrd. Three years later, in November 1716, Christ's Hospital released Robert Biscoe to his mother, Elizabeth Allen, who had apparently remarried, and to "Micajah Perry Esq. to serve Hon. Robert Carter of Rappahannock River, Virginia, merchant."[7]

No record survives of Biscoe's Atlantic voyage or arrival in Virginia. He may have set foot on dock at Carter's Corotoman plantation shortly before Christmas in 1716. Carter's diary provides only scant reference to Biscoe's service. In September 1722, after nearly six years' service, Carter noted that "Bisco prepares cloths for the falls at Pecemds End." This could refer to the provision of winter clothing for slaves at one of Carter's many quarters, indicating that Biscoe's responsibilities included handling and organizing some of the merchandise in Carter's store. On several occasions, Carter mentions "Bisco's book," presumably a ledger he kept of accounts and transactions.[8]

On November 21, 1722, Carter recorded that, "This morning Bisco told me a sad story of Pris & B, I then first heard A.V. was with child."[9] This entry suggests that Biscoe, then 23 and an experienced member of Carter's staff, shared confidences with, as well as the confidence of, his master. Carter must have been dismayed, therefore, when in the month before his indenture was due to expire, Biscoe and another indentured servant teamed up to steal a hogshead of tobacco from him.

Biscoe and Tom Austin, another of Carter's indentured servants, told Captain Richardson of a ship that was loading tobacco for England that a certain hogshead was theirs. Captain Thomas Carter of Lancaster County and a man named McClean found the young men and reported them to Robert Carter. Biscoe had also brought two more hogsheads in Carter's cart, and he had opened a third from Carter's Normands Ford quarter to fill out the other two, which they apparently had planned to sell. The chicanery was discovered on November 7, 1723, just before Biscoe's indenture was to expire. A week later, on November 13, Austin's new indenture was acknowledged in the county court.[10] Both men were required to serve an additional year for Carter, the normal punishment meted out to servants who committed such offenses as running away, stealing, or in the case of young women, bearing a child out of wedlock.

Although Biscoe had to serve additional time, Carter apparently gave him his freedom dues and the customary new suit of clothes before the year was up. During that extra year of servitude, Biscoe may have prepared to become a merchant. In March 1724 he purchased 96 gallons of rum and 166 pounds of sugar through Carter. On November 9, 1724, Carter recorded that "Biscos Tim[e] was out."[11]

In February 1725 Biscoe had three hogsheads of tobacco to sell to Captain Woodward, who was about to make a voyage to England. Biscoe appears in the public record on June 9, 1725, when his letter of attorney to Thomas Edwards and Daniel Carter was proved in Lancaster County Court. Biscoe may have returned to his native land for he next appears in Carter's diary on January 28, 1726, when "Capt Woodward arrived and came ashore with Bisco."[12]

Biscoe was executor for the estate of his "loving friend" Rowland Horne in April 1727. Biscoe and co-executor Henry Horne, brother of the deceased, were also legatees. The value of Horne's estate was recorded as £16.16.2. Horne had a horse, bridle, gun, fiddle, watch, chest of clothing, *Book of Common Prayer*, and a dictionary. He lived in Precinct A of Christ Church Parish and was not a landowner. He may have been, like Biscoe, a former indentured servant who was trying to establish himself in business.[13]

This small legacy may have emboldened Biscoe to ask for the hand of the young woman he loved. She was Elizabeth Lawson of Christ Church Parish, daughter of Henry Lawson, a witness to young Rowland Horne's will. Henry Lawson was from a prominent family in the present-day White Stone area and had served as a justice of the Lancaster County Court and as a vestryman of Christ Church Parish.[14] On May 29, 1727, the bond for the marriage was taken out at Lancaster County court. Henry Lawson gave his consent to his daughter's marriage, and Thomas Edwards, John Steptoe, Jr., and Henry Lawson, Jr., brother of the bride, were securities for the bond.[15] That Biscoe married into a successful and respected family in the parish, in spite of the incident with Carter that could have damaged his reputation, is a tribute to his character.

Robert and Elizabeth Biscoe settled on rented land in Christ Church Parish, a pattern followed by many young couples, especially former indentured servants. In many cases, their goal was to save to purchase land. Biscoe rented 100 acres in Precinct A on a long-term lease from Thomas Lawson, his wife's uncle. This land was part of a 900-acre tract that Lawson had inherited along the Rappahannock River. Biscoe continued to live there until the time of his death.[16] In 1735 Biscoe petitioned the county court for permission to set up gates and draw bars across the main road which led through his plantation from Christ Church to Major Fleet's. His neighbor and father-in-law Henry Lawson requested the same privilege.[17]

Biscoe probably saw himself as a merchant first and farmer second. When the developers, including Robert Carter, drew up plans for Queenstown, a new port town, Carter wrote to Major William Thornton on November 30, 1728, "A neighbor of mine, Robert Biscoe, proposes to buy 3 lots of us that will go at the lowest rates."[18]

Various sources indicate that Biscoe had an active mercantile business. In January 1728, Carter gave Biscoe notes for 13 barrels of corn, on the accounts of McDade, Conne[r] and H. Quary. Biscoe brought suit some 20 times between 1727 and 1736 against customers who had failed to pay him. Persons whom Biscoe took to court ranged from the free black man, Edward Nicken, to gentlemen such as Henry Fleet and Thomas Lee. The amounts in question ranged from 204 pounds of tobacco to the 2,466 pounds of tobacco that Thomas Lee owed Biscoe. He won some judgments and lost others.[19] Biscoe does not seem to have been more litigious than other colonial merchants were. In the absence of banks and credit agencies, merchants had to rely on the courts to help collect accounts due them.

Biscoe occasionally appeared in the records as carrying out some minor public service role. When the processioners for Christ Church Parish carried out their work in 1728, Biscoe witnessed the processioning of land in Precinct A between Richard Chichester, Esq., and John Wrenn.[20] Several friends, relatives, and neighbors called upon him to witness their wills, including Mathias James, Mary Harward [Harwood], Jane Lawson, John Cox, Sr., William Brent, and William Heard. William Brent, in his 1740 will, left Biscoe 400 pounds of tobacco or 40 shillings.[21]

Aware from his own experience and from the custom of the colony that the way to wealth lay in using the labor of others, Biscoe acquired indentured servants. In May 1729, Biscoe signed an indenture with a shoemaker, John Beauford.

This agreement specified that Biscoe would keep the man at his trade and not require him to do agricultural labor in corn or tobacco. For this privilege, Beauford agreed to work one additional year. Biscoe may then have been a dealer in the shoes that his servant made. At the same time Biscoe acquired another servant, Edward Ellis, from Captain Thomas Woodson, a ship's captain who did not live in Lancaster County. The sea captain may have brought Ellis directly from England. He was no Christ's Hospital scholar, for he signed his indenture with a mark, usually the sign of an illiterate person. Nor did he negotiate a favorable working arrangement, so he may have served out his time as an agricultural laborer on the farm that Biscoe leased.[22]

Biscoe also became a slave owner. Several documents between Robert Biscoe and Thomas Edwards concern the slaves Jack and Phillis who had been mortgaged in 1742.[23] Jack may have labored on the farm, and Phillis in the house and the garden. The 1746 tithable list shows two women, Cate and Moll, as slaves of Biscoe. By the time Biscoe died in 1748, the only slave listed on his inventory was Harry, a boy.[24]

There was ample work to do around the Biscoe house and garden, for Robert and Elizabeth Lawson Biscoe had a large family. Their children were John, Mary, Elizabeth, Robert, Sally, Nancy, and William.[25] John, the eldest, was left a cow when he was around 8 to 10 years of age in the 1738 will of Jane Lawson, his aunt. She may have been his godmother as well.[26]

Biscoe's work as a merchant and a farmer can only be said to have brought him a comfortable life and modest success. In another area, however, Biscoe accomplished something that only a tiny handful of Virginians had done in his day. He compiled and published a book. The title page was inscribed: *"The Merchant's Magazine; or, Factors Guide, Containing, Great Variety of plain and easy Tables for speedy Casting up of all Sorts of Merchandize, sold either by Number, Weight or Measure; and for reducing Sterling Money into Currency at sundry Rates; with Tables of Interest and Rebate, and of the Value of Gold and Silver in Vir-*

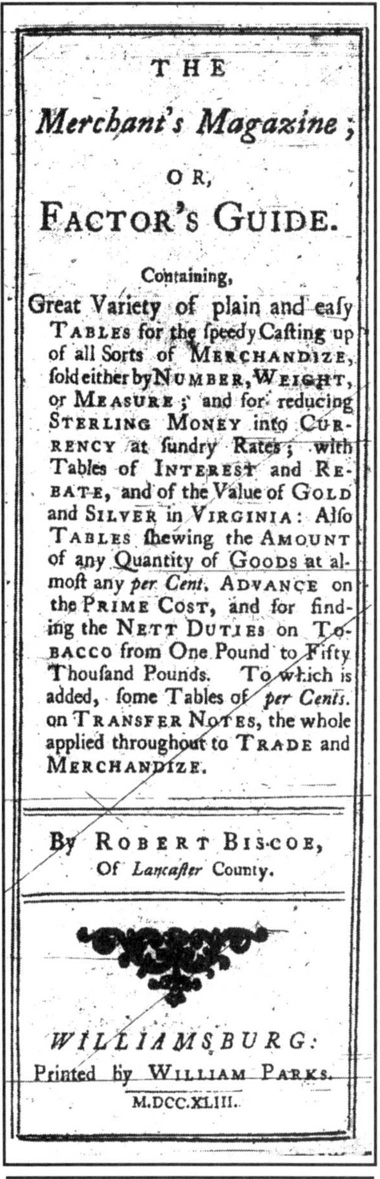

The title page from Robert Biscoe's book, published in Williamsburg in 1743. (Courtesy Colonial Williamsburg Research Library)

ginia: Also Tables shewing the Amount of any Quantity of Goods at almost any per Cent. . . By Robert Biscoe, of Lancaster County. Williamsburg, Printed by William Parks, 1743."

In his preface, Biscoe told his readers that "I have for some Time design'd to publish a Treatise that would be useful to Men concerned in Trade and Commerce; and I thought that if I only collected the best Through out of Authors already extant, and digested them into a proper Method, and illustrated them with Examples, it could not but answer the Design:" He went on to say that "I freely submit the Performance to the Censure of proper Judges, I mean such as have both Skill and Candour enough to judge aright, what the Ignorant and Envious say concerning it, is not to be regarded."[27]

The little book, 3 ½ x 7 inches in size and bound in reddish-brown leather, met with some success, though it is unlikely that Biscoe acquired wealth from its sale. Nonetheless, it appears in many estate inventories. In the 1748 inventory of George Brent, "Biscoe's

Magazine" was appraised at three shillings six pence. George Flower's 1749 will left ". . . to my son George, my book called "Biscoe's Book."[28]

In May of 1747, Biscoe needed cash, so he mortgaged some of his best personal possessions: Harry his slave, two horses, 10 cattle, 10 hogs, six beds, three tables, six leather chairs, a desk, and a chest of drawers, appraised at a total value of £82.4.0. The debt must have been paid before Biscoe died, for these items, except for some livestock, appear on his estate inventory. In January 1748, Biscoe made his will, a simple holographic document without witnesses. He named his wife, Elizabeth, and his son, John, as executors. His wife was to get the three best cows and calves, his sorrel horse, saddle and bridle, two best beds, best chairs, two best dishes, half of the plates, and two best forks. His son John was to have all his wearing apparel. After the debts were paid, the remainder of the estate was to be divided equally among the children. The will was admitted to probate on March 11, 1748. The estate was appraised at £103.11.13.[29]

The inventory of Biscoe's estate, ordered on March 11, 1748, and recorded on May 13, 1748, tells us much about the family and its lifestyle. The five cows, three yearlings, two horses, and eight hogs indicate a small farming operation and provided the opportunity to travel readily with the horses. There was a plough for preparing fields for corn and wheat, and three hilling hoes and three broad hoes for tobacco cultivation.

The shoemaker's tools and supply of upper leather and sole leather recalled the years that Biscoe kept a shoemaker servant in that business. Cotton scales and weights may indicate that crop was raised. The spinning wheel and cards may have been intended for cotton rather than wool, as there is no evidence of sheep.

There were six bedsteads complete with bedding, six tables, five cane back chairs probably in the William & Mary style popular in the 1690s and early 1700s, 11 flag chairs, and six leather chairs, for a total of 22 in the house. There was a

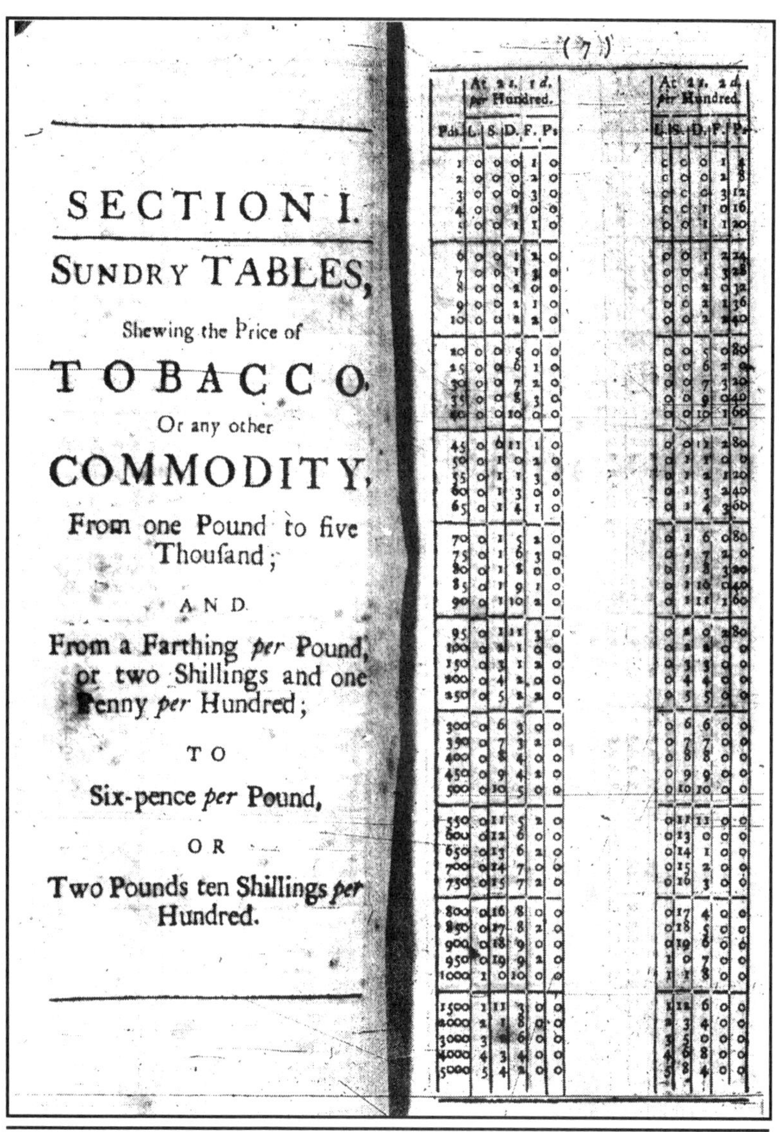

SECTION I.

SUNDRY TABLES,

Shewing the Price of

TOBACCO

Or any other

COMMODITY,

From one Pound to five Thousand;

AND

From a Farthing *per* Pound, or two Shillings and one Penny *per* Hundred;

TO

Six-pence *per* Pound,

OR

Two Pounds ten Shillings *per* Hundred.

Pds.	At 2s. 1d. per Hundred					At 2s. 2d. per Hundred				
	L.	S.	D.	F.	Ps.	L.	S.	D.	F.	Ps.
1	0	0	0	1	0	0	0	0	1	4
2	0	0	0	2	0	0	0	0	2	8
3	0	0	0	3	0	0	0	0	3	12
4	0	0	1	0	0	0	0	1	0	16
5	0	0	1	1	0	0	0	1	1	20
6	0	0	1	2	0	0	0	1	2	24
7	0	0	1	3	0	0	0	1	3	28
8	0	0	2	0	0	0	0	2	0	32
9	0	0	2	1	0	0	0	2	1	36
10	0	0	2	2	0	0	0	2	2	40
20	0	0	5	0	0	0	0	5	0	80
25	0	0	6	1	0	0	0	6	2	0
30	0	0	7	2	0	0	0	7	3	20
35	0	0	8	3	0	0	0	9	0	40
40	0	0	10	0	0	0	0	10	1	60
45	0	0	11	1	0	0	0	11	2	80
50	0	1	0	2	0	0	1	1	0	0
55	0	1	1	3	0	0	1	2	1	20
60	0	1	3	0	0	0	1	3	2	40
65	0	1	4	1	0	0	1	4	3	60
70	0	1	5	2	0	0	1	6	0	80
75	0	1	6	3	0	0	1	7	2	0
80	0	1	8	0	0	0	1	8	3	20
85	0	1	9	1	0	0	1	10	0	40
90	0	1	10	2	0	0	1	11	1	60
95	0	1	11	3	0	0	2	0	2	80
100	0	2	1	0	0	0	2	2	0	0
150	0	3	1	2	0	0	3	3	0	0
200	0	4	2	0	0	0	4	4	0	0
250	0	5	2	2	0	0	5	5	0	0
300	0	6	3	0	0	0	6	6	0	0
350	0	7	3	2	0	0	7	7	0	0
400	0	8	4	0	0	0	8	8	0	0
450	0	9	4	2	0	0	9	9	0	0
500	0	10	5	0	0	0	10	10	0	0
550	0	11	5	2	0	0	11	11	0	0
600	0	12	6	0	0	0	13	0	0	0
650	0	13	6	2	0	0	14	1	0	0
700	0	14	7	0	0	0	15	2	0	0
750	0	15	7	2	0	0	16	3	0	0
800	0	16	8	0	0	0	17	4	0	0
850	0	17	8	2	0	0	18	5	0	0
900	0	18	9	0	0	0	19	6	0	0
950	0	19	9	2	0	1	0	7	0	0
1000	1	0	10	0	0	1	1	8	0	0
1500	1	11	3	0	0	1	12	6	0	0
2000	2	1	8	0	0	2	3	4	0	0
3000	3	2	6	0	0	3	5	0	0	0
4000	4	3	4	0	0	4	6	8	0	0
5000	5	4	2	0	0	5	8	4	0	0

The charts and tables in Robert Biscoe's book were as useful to 18th-century farmers and businessmen as calculators are today. (Courtesy Colonial Williamsburg Research Library) small chest, a large trunk, a small cabinet, an old chest of drawers, an old desk and three mirrors. Twelve pictures, half of which were framed, helped decorate the rooms. The Biscoes had no silver, but they did own a number of pewter objects including a caudle cup, spoons, a teapot, a chamber pot, and 28 pounds of old pewter.

Most interesting, considering the education with which Biscoe was blessed, was his library. It was surely one of the largest in the parish, outside of the wealthy planters like Carter, Conway, and Gordon. He owned a great Bible, a small Bible, a large dictionary, Mersers and Webbs Abridgements, 54 books with no titles indicated, and a supply of 48 copies of Biscoe's own book, the *Merchants Magazine*.[30]

Biscoe's education had given him opportunity for success in life that eluded his fishmonger father. To some extent, he had realized that success. He had married well into a respectable family above his own birth status. He maintained a house that was larger and better furnished than those of many of his contemporaries in Christ Church Parish. He had purchased the labor of indentured servants and of two slaves to assist him, one of whom he still owned at his death. And he achieved something that few colonial Americans managed, the publication of a book of his own.

Yet other marks of success in Virginia eluded him. He never became a landowner, a primary indicator of success and a prerequisite for political participation. Biscoe never held public office, even the modest positions of constable or processioner. The single most valuable item in Biscoe's estate was his "negro boy Harry" at £35, fully one-third of the total estate value, yet one slave was not enough to bring economic success.

Virginia was a good opportunity, but Biscoe only modestly provided for his family. In April 1756, his widow, Elizabeth Biscoe, made a deed of gift dividing her entire estate equally among all her children, John Biscoe, Mary Hunton, Elizabeth Biscoe, Robert Biscoe, Sally Biscoe, Nancy Biscoe, and William Biscoe, while reserving for herself a life estate.[31]

In 1756, Elizabeth Biscoe arranged an indenture for her second son, Robert, to John Hathaway until he was 21. Hathaway was to teach young Robert how to read and write and train him as a house joiner. Five years later, she indentured the youngest child, William, to John Lock to learn the trade of tailor.[32]

Robert Biscoe founded a family that remained a part of the Lancaster County community for several generations after its immigrant patriarch died. His book was a significant accomplishment, and was well regarded, for examples of inventories of other Virginians occasionally counted "Biscoe's book" or "Biscoe's Magazine" among the possessions.

ENDNOTES

[1]Peter Wilson Coldham, *Child Apprentices in America from Christ's Hospital, London, 1617-1778* (Baltimore: Genealogical Publishing Company, 1989), 36. A baptismal record for Robert Biscoe has not been found. Holy Trinity was the parish church from which he entered Christ's Hospital 10 years later. Del Moore of the Rockefeller Library at Colonial Williamsburg directed the attention of the Parish Profile Researchers to published materials about Robert Biscoe and Christ's Hospital.

[2]Clifford Dowdy, *The Virginia Dynasties: The Emergence of "King" Carter and the Golden Age* (New York: Bonanza Books, 1969), 173.

[3]The opening of the records of Christ's Hospital to researchers in the 1980s made possible a new understanding of the significant connections between this school and the American colonies. Two articles in the *Colonial Williamsburg* magazine in 1988 emphasize those ties. The admission register in 1709 records the entry of Robert Biscoe. He remained at the school until November 1716. Harold B. Gill, Jr., "Apprentices from Christ's Hospital Make Good in America," *Colonial Williamsburg*, Autumn 1988 and J.E. Morpurgo, "A Thing Without Parallel: Christ's Hospital and America," *Colonial Williamsburg*, Autumn 1988.

[4]Morpurgo, "A Thing Without Parallel: Christ's Hospital and America," 7-9.

[5]Ibid., 11-12.

[6]Gill, "Apprentices from Christ's Hospital Make Good in America," 15-17.

[7]Quoted in Coldham, 36.

[8]Robert Carter Diary 1722-1728, 25 September 1722. Transcribed from a partially corrected, typed transcript property of the University of Virginia Library, lent by Francis L. Berkeley, solely for reference and research use by the Historic Christ Church Foundation volunteers.

[9]Ibid., 21 November 1722.

[10]Ibid., 7 November, 13 November 1723. See also Lancaster County Court Order Book 7:129.

[11]Ibid., 16 November 1723, 18 March, 9 November 1724.

[12]Ibid., 28 January 1725/26.

[13]Lancaster County Will Book 10: 544, 547, 552. Rowland Horne's will, written on 1 April 1727, was entered for probate on 12 April. Witnesses to the will were Samuel Ball and Henry Lawson. Appraisers of the estate were Ezekiel Gilbert, William Brent, and William Martin.

[14]See Lawson family chapter in this book, and FHCCRF – Lawson Family File.

[15]Lancaster County Marriage Register, 29 May 1727. Elizabeth Lawson had a cousin, Joanna, who married John Steptoe, Jr., one of the securities to this marriage bond, also in 1727.

[16]Thomas Lawson will, Lancaster County Deed Book 14:147. Lawson's 1747 will stated that after Robert Biscoe's lease expired, the 100 acres were to be sold to the highest bidder. Biscoe died the following January.

[17]Lancaster County Court Order Book 8:137.

[18]Robert Carter to William Thornton, 30 November 1728. Robert Carter Letterbook #3, October 1728-May 1730, Virginia Historical Society; Letters of Robert Carter transcribed. 5:14. FHCCRF.

[19]Suits for which judgment was obtained in 1727 are found in Lancaster County Court Order Book 7:254, 279, 285, 308, and 314. Suits for which judgment was obtained in 1731 are to be found in Lancaster Court County Order Book 8:32, 42, 43, 76, 107, 108, 111, 146, 295, and 302.

[20]Processioners Returns Christ Church Parish, 15 June 1728, 39a.

[21]John Cox, Sr., Lancaster County Will Book 13:7; Mary Harwood, Will Book 13:71; Jane Lawson, Will Book 13:71; Mathias James Will Book 13:159; William Brent Will Book 13:177; William Heard, Will Book 14:35.

[22]The two indentures with servants John Beauford and Edward Ellis are recorded in Lancaster County Deed and Will Book 12:104, 105.

[23]Lancaster County Court Order Book, 13 January 1737, 8:13; 14 May 1742, Order Book 8:342, 345.

[24]Lancaster County Deed and Will Book 14:193.

[25]The Biscoe children are named in a deed of gift from their widowed mother dated 14 April 1756. Lancaster County Deed and Will Book 15:244.

[26]Will of Jane Lawson, Lancaster County Will Book 13:111.

[27]Biscoe, *The Merchant's Magazine*, "The Preface."

[28]Inventory of George Brent, 1748, Lancaster County Will Book 14:220-222; Will of George Flowers, 1749 Will Book 14:269.

[29]Lancaster County Court Order Book 9:151; Deed and Will Book 14:180.

[30]Robert Biscoe inventory and appraisal, recorded 13 May 1748, Lancaster County Deed and Will Book 14:193.

[31]Elizabeth Biscoe, Deed of Gift, Lancaster County Deed and Will Book 15:244.

[32]Indenture of Robert Biscoe, 21 May 1756, Lancaster Court Order Book 10:422; Indenture of William Biscoe, 17 April 1761, Ibid., 11:315.

Priscilla Palmer Reeves
A Parishioner in Trouble

From the high vantage point of his home, Richard Chichester, Esq., could survey the entrance to Carters Creek and the Rappahannock River beyond and with his spy glass identify the incoming ships and those at anchor – very convenient for the Collector of the Rappahannock. Chichester was appointed to this governmental naval office in 1699 and held it for many years.[1] The appointment was one of several positions of leadership which he held in Lancaster County.

The promontory from which Chichester could survey his Chesapeake world was part of a beautiful 100-acre tract of land he had purchased from Nicholas Wren in 1702.[2] Situated as it was near the mouth of Carters Creek and just a short distance from the entrance to the Rappahannock River, the plantation was the ideal locale for a person whose job was to monitor the river traffic. Additionally, just across the water toward the mouth of the creek were the home and wharves of the county's most powerful man, Robert Carter.

Eventually Chichester's small plantation wound up in the hands of Priscilla Palmer Reeves, a woman whose poignant story speaks volumes about the life of women in colonial Virginia and the interaction of people from the many different levels of society in Christ Church Parish. The story of Priscilla is also the story of how a local gentleman and a mother and daughter became intertwined with a piece of land that was known long after the trio was gone as "Priscilla's." The explanation of how this piece of land came to be designated as such has come to light through the Lancaster County record books, but some tantalizing details have been lost to the mists of time.

Chichester's land meshed well with a world dominated by water transportation. In fact, his land was surrounded by water on three sides. The fourth side, the land boundary, was often in dispute. Traveling to the nearby glebe or to his good

The Chichester family crest shows a bird with its wings extended and holding a snake in its beak. (Courtesy "Virginia Heraldica")

friend John Turbervile's house meant a long trip inland by horseback over a horse bridge built specifically for residents traveling overland. However, most convenient trips were by water. Small boats could navigate far up the many creeks. Christ Church could be reached easily by following the western branch of Carters Creek, past John Wren's land then up the prong past the glebe to the church landing. A trip to Carter's plantation meant several tiring hours by horseback but only a few minutes by boat.[3]

Chichester descended from a prominent gentry family from Devon, England. The family traced its roots to Sir Roger Chichester, who was knighted at Calais in the 14th century. Richard Chichester of Lancaster County was the second son of John Chichester of Widworthy and his wife, Margaret Ware. He was born on March 5, 1657 and baptized 11 days later at Silverton. Because his father was a knight, Richard was entitled to use esquire after his name, which he did on most documents in Lancaster County. Of his youth and education, we know nothing, but sometime before 1681 he married Anna and the couple had a son, John, who was baptized at Widworthy on May 10, 1681. The Chichester family seemed drawn to the American colonies. According to tradition, Richard's older brother, Sir John Chichester, was murdered in Liverpool as he waited to board a ship for America. That same story pins the murder on Sir John's servant working in concert with the innkeeper where Chichester was staying.[4]

Richard Chichester's life in Lancaster County during the early 18th century must have been filled with the duties of public life but privately may very well have been quite lonely for a man in his early forties. He apparently had no wife in Virginia during his first years in the colony, but whether she ever came to America or had died in England is uncertain. His son grew up and gained an education in Britain. Abating that loneliness was the friendship of Amie (Amy) Palmer[5] and her daughter Priscilla. The exact relationship between Palmer and Chichester has never been discovered. Both women were important enough to him that he remembered them with gifts while he was alive and later in his will. Amie may have been a relative of Chichester either by blood or marriage or she may have been a relative of one of his friends. She may have kept house for the lonely government official who appears to have had no close family nearby in Virginia. Such a housekeeping arrangement would not have been uncommon in the 18th century, when women were deemed indispensable in running households. Perhaps the arrangement began on that level and developed into something deeper. Priscilla's presence increases the mystery as the identity of her father has never been determined. Was Amie Palmer a young widow with a small child who was brought under the paternal wing of one of the parish elite or was Priscilla the illegitimate child of Chichester?

If the Palmers filled a void in Chichester's life, it was something for which he was always grateful. Eventually he would repay the debt through his powers as a local official and as a member of the area gentry. Chichester's loneliness abated somewhat in the final two decades of his life. At some

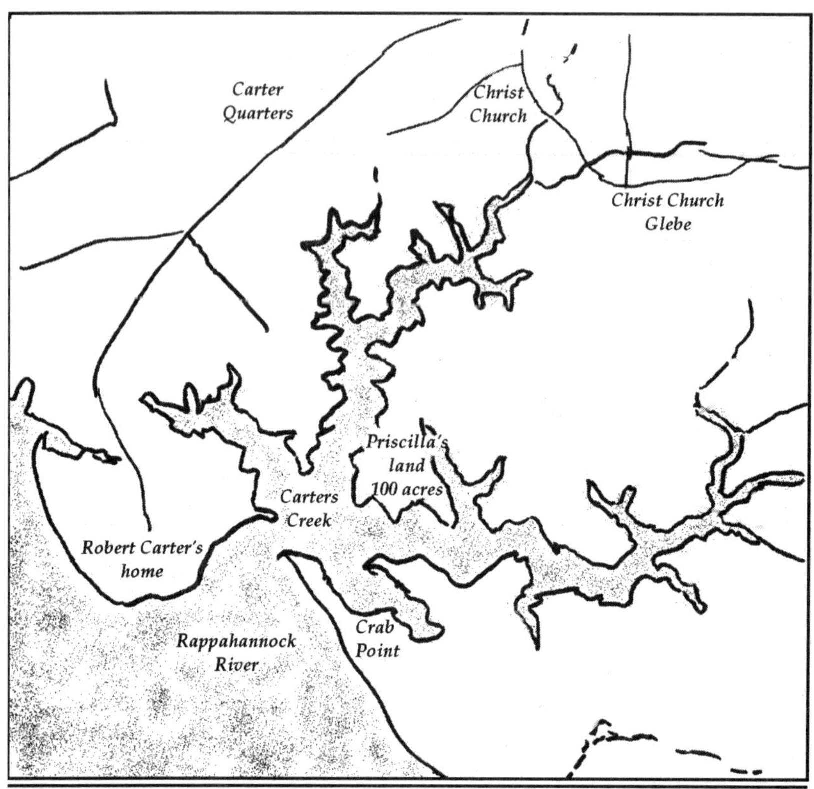

This map shows the location of Priscilla Palmer Reeves' land on Carters Creek.

point before 1710 his grown son, John, arrived in Virginia from England, followed by his daughter-in-law, Elizabeth, and their small son, Richard, who was four or five years old. Perhaps his family's arrival spurred him to expand his land holdings, for in 1710 he purchased 500 acres in White Chapel Parish, a different parish (although served by the same minister) but still in Lancaster County along the Rappahannock River.[6] John Chichester eventually followed in his father's footsteps as a public servant, for in 1721 he was described as the King's attorney.[7] The Chichester family togetherness did not last long. After a few years, Elizabeth became ill and returned to England with her son Richard. In 1728, John Chichester became gravely ill with gout and died. His father, Richard, administered the estate of his 47-year-old son. After the death of his son, Richard wrote to England requesting that his grandson, Richard, be sent to Virginia to live with him. The two Richard Chichesters, grandfather and grandson, lived together until the death of the elder in May of 1734.[8]

Before he removed himself to White Chapel Parish, Richard Chichester took steps to ensure that Amie and Priscilla Palmer were provided for throughout their lives. Whether or not they were living on the 100-acre tract of land before 1710 is uncertain — although most likely they were already sharing the living space there with Chichester — but they almost certainly were there sometime after 1710. Chichester had an unusual conveyance drawn up. Through a deed of gift he gave Amie Palmer his land but retained a life estate for himself. He used his friend John Turbervile as the administrator of his wishes and trustee for the tract of land. The agreement involving the 100-acre plantation was actually between Chichester and Turbervile, and included "the land and all houses, barns, stables and edifices pertaining to the tract in Christ Church Parish whereon Richard Chichester, Esqr. now liveth." Chichester retained the land for himself during his natural life and then stipulated that it was to pass to Amie Palmer "during the time she shall live sole and unmarried." After her death it was to pass to "Priscilla Palmer and heirs of her body lawfully begotten." If Priscilla Palmer had no heirs then the land was to revert to Chichester's son, John Chichester.[9]

A few months later, in December of 1710, Richard Chichester had another legal contract drawn up, this time between himself and Priscilla, who was surely a young child at the time. For the nominal sum of 20 shillings sterling, Chichester sold to Priscilla two slaves, Jack and Judith, who were each about a year old.[10] While this transaction initially appears odd, it was not uncommon for upper class families to give young slaves to young white children. Not only did this teach the white children the intricacies and responsibilities of slave ownership, but it was often a situation created with the hope that by placing black and white children together, lifelong companions and trusted servants could be created.[11]

Whether Chichester remained on his Christ Church Parish land after his flurry of legal activity in 1710 or removed to White Chapel Parish immediately after recording his deed of gift for Amie Palmer is uncertain, but by 1719 he quit his residence in the parish. By then, Chichester's eye had caught notice of Ann Fox, the wealthy widow of William Fox. They married in 1719, and the 62-year-old Chichester settled down with his bride in White Chapel Parish.[12]

Maybe marriage between Amie Palmer and Richard Chichester was never an option because of their vast differences in social status or perhaps no romantic involvement between the two ever existed.[13] However, Chichester evidently thought enough of the two Palmer women to ensure that they had a place to live out their lives, and by doing that he placed them among the small number of women who ever held land in the parish in the first half of the 18th century.

The land on which the Palmers came to reside was valuable in terms of accessibility by boat and because of its close proximity to one of the richest and most powerful men in Lancaster and probably in all of Virginia. Robert Carter's plantation and wharves were more akin to a small community than a farm. There the Palmer women could meet and mingle with persons from all levels of society from slaves, indentured servants, and seafaring men from faraway lands to members of the colonial gentry. This could have been where Priscilla met and became involved with Billy, a slave owned by Carter.

Unfortunately for Priscilla, her indiscretions brought her squarely up against Carter and she threatened him where it hurt — certainly in his pocketbook and perhaps personally as well. That Carter knew Priscilla is clear from his diary entry of November 21, 1722: "This morning Bisco told me a sad Storey of Pris & B, I then first heard A. V. was with Child."[14] Carter's oblique reference is to two of his workforce, one a slave carpenter named Mulatto Billy and one an indentured servant named Ann Vittey, both of whom were going to be parents of illegitimate children. The first part of the entry involved Priscilla. The messenger of the news was Robert Biscoe, a trusted indentured bookkeeper of Carter who had gained his master's confidence.

Women who bore illegitimate children in 18th-century Virginia could suffer harsh punishment under the letter of the law, although in reality the punishments were often less severe. Not only were their indiscretions considered morally depraved, but from a practical standpoint they were also increasing the taxpayers' burden by adding a person to society whose needs would probably be met through the public coffers. Because the circumstances of Priscilla, a free white woman, and Ann, an indentured white woman, were different, they faced different punishments under the law. An indentured servant convicted of fornication could be forced to pay 500 pounds of tobacco or receive 25 lashes on the bare back or serve two months in prison. In addition, six months were added to the term of servitude. If an out-of-wedlock child was the result of such behavior, either a year was added to the servitude or the offending servant had to pay her master 1,000 pounds of tobacco.[15]

The law put a different set of punishments on people like Priscilla. Not only did Priscilla face the potential of the same 500 pounds of tobacco/25 lashes/two months imprisonment sentence, but her involvement with a slave meant that she had also tampered with another man's property and had crossed racial lines with her indiscretion. In such cases the law stated: "That if any English woman being free shall have a bastard child by any negro or mulatto, she pay the sume of fifteen pounds sterling, within one moneth after such bastard child be born, to the church wardens of the parish where she shall be delivered of such child, and in default of such payment she shall be taken into the possession of the said Church wardens and disposed of for five years."

The law further stated:

> . . .the said fine of fifteen pounds, or whatever the
> woman shall be disposed of for, shall be paid, one third
> part to their majesties for and towards the support of
> the government and the contingent charges thereof,
> and the one other third part to the use of the parish
> where the offence is committed, and the other third
> part to the informer, and that such bastard child be
> bound out as a servant by the said Church wardens
> until he or she shall attaine the age of thirty yeares. . . .[16]

At some point after he found out about the pregnancy involving his slave Billy and Priscilla, Carter reported the offenders to the authorities. He probably did so for two reasons. First, he was a churchwarden and there was a moral and financial obligation to report the offense. Secondly, history had proved that in many such cases the couple attempted to flee the area and if that happened, Carter would lose the labor of his slave.

Before the birth of her illegitimate son, Priscilla had been arrested by the Lancaster County sheriff, who happened to be none other than Richard Chichester, by now married and living in White Chapel Parish. According to records, Chichester held her in custody at the "county gaol" until the baby's birth on March 26.[17]

Shortly after she gave birth, Priscilla paid her £15 fine as stipulated by the law. The order books do not record what happened to the child, but, by law, he should have been bound out as a servant until the age of 30. About a decade later, the estate inventory drawn up at Robert Carter's death listed "Mulatto Billy, carpenter, and Johnny his son, about age 8."[18] If Johnny was indeed the result of Billy and Priscilla's tryst, he would have still owed the Carter family about 20 years of service.

Priscilla's predicament was not an isolated incident in the parish or the county. In 1722 in the county as a whole there were at least four similar cases of county women bearing bastards, including one from Christ Church Parish, while

1723 saw half a dozen Christ Church Parish women charged. Interesting to note in reference to this was the swearing in during 1722 of Richard Chichester as Sheriff of Lancaster County and Joseph Carter as Under Sheriff. Both may have had sympathy toward such women "in trouble," as Chichester is suspected by some researchers as having fathered Priscilla illegitimately and Joseph Carter is recorded as having confessed, on the very day he was sworn in as Chichester's assistant, to fathering an illegitimate child.[19] A survey of the court order books in 1722 and 1723 shows that no whippings or imprisonments were ordered on any of the charged women despite several instances of late payments of fines.

The circumstances of Priscilla's case ensured that she would have to go head-to-head in court with the powerful Robert Carter. Indeed, on May 8, 1723, just weeks after Priscilla gave birth to a base-born son in the Lancaster County jail, Carter filed a complaint against her for having "an Intreague with a slave of his named mulatto Billy & being catchd abed with his sd slave in his negro quarter whereby he has reason to believe he is a great suffered & that if the sd Intreague is not prevented in time the sd Priscilla will run away with his sd slave. . . ."[20]

As a result of the complaint, Priscilla was ordered to appear in court with a trunk of her belongings. Among the items in the trunk was a blanket which Carter said belonged to him. Perhaps Carter thought Billy brought the blanket with him to Priscilla's house during a period of five days that she "had harboured the sd slave," or he might have been accusing her of stealing it from his quarters. Witnesses noted that Priscilla had "frequent confederacy with him [Billy] & was cacht in bed with him as aforesd." For her part, Priscilla denied that Carter owned the blanket, saying that it belonged, instead, to a woman in Middlesex County.[21]

At first glance it seems remarkable that Carter, perhaps the richest man in Virginia, would quibble over the ownership of a blanket. However, the real reason for the court showdown probably had nothing to do with the blanket but more to do with the fact that he feared his slave would run off with Priscilla, thus depriving him of a very valuable piece of property.

Although the court found Priscilla guilty of the charges of intrigue with Billy, her punishment was relatively light. She was ordered to pay Carter 150 pounds of tobacco and be "kept in custody of the sd Sherif of this County til she give security for her good behavior for one year and a day."[22] The blanket matter was eventually dismissed despite the fact that the alleged owner of the blanket in Middlesex County denied knowing anything of the item.[23] One final detail that had to be worked out was the matter of how Priscilla's £15 fine should be allotted. Because the "crime" took place in Christ Church Parish, Priscilla lived in Christ Church, and a Christ Church warden had made the complaint, Carter wanted the money for the use of his vestry, while vestry members of St. Mary's White Chapel Parish, where the birth had taken place and where Priscilla was to serve out her sentence, wanted the fine to help care for their poor. Carter argued that technically the two parishes were one and the money should go to his parish. The White Chapel representatives disagreed but offered to give some money to Christ Church. The entire matter eventually went unresolved after the court dismissed it.[24]

For her part, Priscilla escaped almost unscathed. She had to pay fines of 150 pounds of tobacco and £15 sterling. Furthermore, she was remanded into the hands of Chichester, her friend and possibly her kinsman. Did Chichester intercede on her behalf and convince the court to go easy on Priscilla? The answer will never be known. During her 366-day probation with Chichester, she almost got into trouble for not attending church for two months. However, Chichester once again interceded and the church wardens dismissed the case against her because the absence occurred "at the time she is supposed to have absented from the church in the sherif's custody."[25]

Certainly Chichester and others told her that the continuance of such behavior would not be tolerated and probably warned her that she had better amend her ways. Clearly

Priscilla heeded those warnings because in August 1724, shortly after her probation was over, she married Eaton Reeves, the son of John Reeves of St. Mary's White Chapel Parish.[26] The marriage register lists Priscilla's residence as St. Mary's White Chapel which would have been the case if she were staying, at least temporarily, with Chichester.

Priscilla and Eaton had one son, named John, who was born not before 1726. In 1745 John Reeves, described as the son of Eaton and son at law of Priscilla, was apprenticed to Absalom Mahon to learn the weaving trade until he reached the age of 21.[27] It was this son John and not the illegitimate son Johnny who stood to inherit Chichester's land as a result of the 1710 deed because that document stated that the land would pass to Priscilla's heirs only if they were legitimate.

By the time Chichester died in 1734, Amie Palmer, Priscilla's mother, had also died. Priscilla, who by this time appears to have become a solid member of society, was well remembered by Chichester. From his will, she received an annual allowance of 500 pounds of tobacco, a hair trunk marked with the initials AAC, and the contents of his house in Christ Church Parish. The latter was explained in the will:

> I give and bequeath unto the before named Priscilla Reeves daughter of Amie Palmer dec'd what goods I have in my house in Christ Church Parish in the county of Lancaster in Virginia at my decease, the house and land being already made over to her and her children lawfully begotten during their natural lives after my decease.[28]

There is no way of knowing if the Reeves family was established on the property before Chichester's death in 1734, but there is also no reason to doubt that they were there. Extant processioners returns from the men who walked the local boundary lines are of little help. From 1711 to 1727 the tract of land is listed in the name of Richard Chichester. In 1735, the year after Chichester's death, the processioners described the land as being in the possession of Eaton Reeves. As long as Eaton was alive, his wife Priscilla had no legal rights separate from her husband. Therefore, the land that she inherited belonged to her husband.

Eaton Reeves appears to have died sometime after 1735. In February of that year, he was involved in a lawsuit with a merchant named James Hubbard, who claimed Reeves owed him £2:8:2. Also in 1735 he is listed on the processioners returns. The next mention of the Reeves name associated with that piece of land occurred in 1739, when the processioners recorded that they walked the line between "Pressila Reeves" and John Wren. Priscilla's name is associated with the land again in 1743.[29]

Sometime between 1735 and 1739, Eaton Reeves died which meant that Priscilla could reassume a legal identity. She had no qualms about exercising her rights. Whether it was because she had enjoyed the legal and social protection of Chichester or whether she had regained the public's confidence through upright behavior, Priscilla's reputation does not appear to have been besmirched by her brush with the law two decades earlier. In April 1742, she took Thomas Bridgeford to court for 357½ pounds of tobacco she felt he owed her. The court listened to both sides of the story and then dismissed the case. However the court did request that Reeves reimburse Bridgeford his court costs.[30]

Priscilla's story closed sometime after May 1742 and before 1755, when the processioners described her tract of land as belonging to John Reeves, her son.[31] In September of 1756, John Reeves sold his 100 acres of land near the glebe to Henry Tapscott. In 1772 when Tapscott sold the same tract of land to Bailey George, the land was described as "All that tract which formerly belonged to Richard Chichester, Esq. and by him given to Priscilla Palmer by indenture 12 March 1710 and on her death it descended to her heir and son at law John Reeves who conveyed the same to Henry Tapscott."[32]

When John Reeves sold the land he ended his family's connection to that 100-acre tract. Priscilla's story is much more than that of a headstrong young woman and an aging member of the area gentry. In 1773 a brief statement in a deed book made it clear that Priscilla had made her mark on the area. The plantation which she and her mother had owned was by now known simply as "Priscilla's."[33]

Today, a gracious resort known for a long time as the Tide's Inn is located adjacent to the property known for years simply as Priscilla's. The story behind the land's name is a fascinating one, filled with 18th-century social mores and ideas of justice and punishment that we can hardly fathom. It is also a story about a special relationship between Chichester and two women he cared a great deal about — Amie and Priscilla.

ENDNOTES

[1] At the 1699 council, Chichester's predecessor was ordered to turn over all the books, bonds, cocketts, certificates, writings, papers, and all other things that were part of the office. *Executive Journals of the Council of Colonial Virginia*, vol. II, edited by H.R. McIlwaine (Richmond: The Virginia State Library, 1927), Council at James City, 22 February 1699, 41-45.

[2] Lancaster County Deed Book 9:26.

[3] FHCCRF - Parish Profile archives.

[4] *Virginia Heraldica*, edited by William Armstrong Crozier (Baltimore: Genealogical Publishing Co., Inc., 1978, originally published in 1908), 77-78 and Dr. Joseph Lyon Miller, "Captain Thomas Carter and His Descendants," *William and Mary Quarterly*, July 1908, 284-285.

[5] Very few clues exist in regard to Amie (Amy) Palmer. Although Palmers resided in the parish in the 17th century, it is not known if there was a kinship between them and Amie Palmer or even if Palmer was Amie's maiden name. The only other document, outside of the ones cited in this article, that mentions Amie Palmer is the will of Mary Phipps of Christ Church Parish. Palmer is a legatee, described as "my beloved friend," while Chichester is described as a friend and the executor of Phipps' estate. Palmer was given the responsibility of taking over the indenture of servant Elizabeth Hall and then making sure that Hall received a cow and calf, an iron pot, a spinning wheel, wool cards, two religious books, a red-gilded leather trunk, and a suit of woolen clothes when her indenture was finished. Lancaster County Will Book 10:49.

[6] Chichester purchased the 500 acres from Robert Hall, Lancaster County Deed Book 9:321, 10 May 1710.

[7] On 8 November 1721, John Chichester received 1,000 pounds of tobacco for a year's service as the King's Attorney. Lancaster County Court Order Book 7:16, 8 November 1721.

[8] Lancaster County Will Book 13:318.

[9] Lancaster County Deed and Will Book 9:365, 12 March 1710.

[10]Lancaster County Deed and Will Book 9:343, 14 December 1710.

[11]Philip D. Morgan, *Slave Counterpoint: Black Culture in the Eighteenth-Century Chesapeake & Lowcountry* (University of North Carolina Press, 1998), 379-380.

[12]Lancaster County Marriage Register, "Richard Chichester to Ann Fox, widow of William Fox, dec'd. 11 July 1719." Ann Chichester, whose will was written in February 1725, appears to have died in late 1729. Her will was recorded on 10 December 1729, and the inventory of her estate was returned in May 1730. Lancaster County Will Book 12:172.

[13]Palmer's date of death is also a mystery as she left no will, but it had occurred by 1734 when Chichester describes her as deceased in his own will. Lancaster County Will Book 12:310.

[14]Robert Carter Diary 1722-1728, 21 November 1722. Transcribed from a partially corrected, typed transcript property of the University of Virginia Library, lent by Francis L. Berkeley, solely for reference and research use by the Historic Christ Church Foundation volunteers.

[15]*The Laws of Virginia: Being a supplement to Hening's The Statutes at Large, 1700-1750*, compiled by Waverly K. Winfree (Richmond: the Virginia State Library, 1971), September 1696, 139-140.

[16]Ibid., 87. In 1727, nearly five years after Priscilla Palmer's difficult situation, the law was changed to eliminate the imprisonment clause and the "disposed for five years" clause.

[17]Lancaster County Court Order Book 7:98, 8 May 1723.

[18]Robert Carter estate inventory, 1732, p. 34. FHCCRF.

[19]Lancaster County Court Order Book 7:43, 48, 50, 52, 56, 62, 71, 91, 98, 102, 115, and 119.

[20]Lancaster County Court Order Book entries pertaining to Robert Carter, Lancaster County, Virginia, compiled by Christine Adams Jones. FHCCRF. Lancaster County Court Order Book 7:100, 8 May 1723.

[21]Ibid.

[22]Ibid.

[23]Ibid., 113, 10 July 1723.

[24]Ibid., 7:98-99, 8 May 1723.

[25]Lancaster County Court Order Book 7:131, 13 November 1723.

[26]Lancaster County Marriage Register, Eaton Reeves to Priscilla Palmer, August 1724.

[27]Lancaster County Court Order Book 9:66.

[28]Lancaster Deed and Will Book 12:310.

[29]Christ Church Parish Processioners returns, 1711, 1719, 1727, 1735, 1739, 1743, and 1747.

[30]Lancaster Court Court Order Book 8:337, 9 April 1742 and 8:343, 14 May 1742.

[31]Christ Church Parish Processioners Returns, 1755.

[32]Lancaster County Deed Book 19:48, 18 June 1772.

[33]Lancaster County Deed Book 19:76.

THE LAWSON FAMILY

Some Lancaster County families are remembered because one of their members was an outstanding figure in some respect such as political power, wealth, notorious conduct, or religious rectitude. Other families are notable for a long record of solid citizenship. The Lawson family of Lancaster was one such example.

The Lawson family traced its appearance in Lancaster County to two brothers, Epaphroditus and Rowland Lawson, who were among the first settlers of the region. Like several other early settlers in the area that was to become Lancaster County, including John Carter, father of Robert "King" Carter, the Lawsons settled along the Nansemond River when they first came to Virginia.[1] From a 1642 patent, we know that Epaphroditus claimed headrights for the transportation of himself and William Lawson, Lettice Lawson, and Rowland Lawson.[2]

Beginning in 1649, Epaphroditus Lawson focused his interests northward on the Rappahannock River. In September of that year, he received a grant of 700 acres on the Rappahannock at the mouth of Slaughters Creek, which divided his land from that of John Carter. In May 1650, he received 2,000 acres on the south side of the river for transporting 40 persons. In 1650, Governor William Berkeley made two separate grants to Epaphroditus Lawson for 1,000 acres and for 700 acres. At his death, he left the 1,000-acre tract to his daughter, Elizabeth, an only child and wife of Robert Davis. This land passed out of the Lawson line. The 700-acre tract was sold and became part of the glebe for Christ Church Parish. The unusual name of Epaphroditus continued in the Lawson family because John (1) Lawson, son of Rowland (1), gave it to one of his sons.[3]

Rowland Lawson, the other brother, received a grant from Governor Berkeley in 1651 for 1,300 acres on the north side of the Rappahannock at the eastward side of the mouth of Cherry Point Creek. This land came to Rowland in two parcels. The first consisted of 900 acres assigned to Rowland from his brother Epaphroditus. The second was 400 acres that Rowland received for the transport of eight persons into the colony.[4] One other patent was recorded for this Rowland Lawson, in 1654, for 400 acres on the south side of the Rappahannock for transporting eight persons.[5] This first Rowland Lawson was married to Lettice Wale. They were the parents of three sons, Rowland, Henry, and John, and two daughters, Elizabeth and Letitia.[6] Rowland Lawson was a leading citizen of early Lancaster County, serving as a justice from 1652 to 1655. He died in 1661.

Rowland (2), the eldest son, was the principal heir of this estate, inheriting 1,300-1,400 acres that stretched along the Rappahannock near its entry into the Chesapeake Bay. In deeds of gift a decade apart, Rowland (2) gave what appears to be the 400-acre tract to his brothers. Half of this tract went in 1669 to his brother Henry, with the provision that if Henry should die before reaching the age of 21, the land would return to Rowland (2). He gave the other half of this 400 acres in 1678 to his brother John. Henry apparently died before reaching majority with the land reverting to Rowland (2).[7]

John Lawson married Mary Kilby or Kirby and was father to Epaphroditus (2), named for John's uncle, Epaphroditus (1). It was in this new son's family line that the name Epaphroditus was perpetuated. John Lawson's other children were John (2) and a daughter, Catherine (d. 1722).[8] This line, that of a younger son, had more limited economic expectations. After John Lawson died, his widow Mary Kilby/Kirby Lawson married George Harwood, who made provision in his will for the sons of his wife's first husband, Epaphroditus and John. Rowland (2) disposed of another tract, 24 acres comprising the Broken Islands at the mouth of Mosquito Creek, to his son Rowland (3) in 1699.[9]

Rowland (2) Lawson wrote his will on the last day of the

year on the old calendar, a date that we recognize as March 24, 1705. It was probated in September 1706. Lawson still maintained business ties in England, which he left to the care of his son, Rowland.[10] The seal on Rowland Lawson's will bears a chevron between three martlets. According to Burke, these arms belong to Lawson of Burgh Hall, Yorkshire and of Cramlington, Northumberland, and Longherst, Northumberland.[11] Rowland Lawson's use of this seal indicates his kinship identification with a gentry family from the north of England.

Rowland (2) Lawson and his wife Ann, whose maiden name may have been Chaplin, were the parents of two sons, Rowland (3) and Henry, named for Rowland's deceased brother. By the terms of his father's will, Henry received the western part of Rowland's land, beginning at Creeple (also Cripple or Cripeld) Hill. It is presumed that this land was the same acreage (200 acres) that had been given in 1669 to the deceased brother Henry. This gift is illustrative of the family cohesiveness that marked the Lawson family's early history in the parish. No specific allotment to Rowland (3) is mentioned in the will, but he was the sole executor and seems to have been the principal heir, and was certainly of age by 1704.

In 1712, this third Rowland Lawson to live on the original Lancaster County grant deeded an additional 50 acres to his brother, Henry.[12] The deed identified the land as being "neer the head of a valley that makes out from Rappa: River known by the name of YE HORSE VALLEY." This Henry Lawson married Mary Sallard Kelly, daughter of Simon Sallard and widow of John Kelly. In the 1721 Rent Roll for Lord Fairfax's Northern Neck, Henry Lawson was shown holding 375 acres. This included the 200 acres inherited from his father, 125 acres that belonged to his wife, Mary, and the 50 acres deeded by his brother, Rowland.[13] Henry and Mary Sallard Kelly Lawson had three sons, Rowland, who seems to have died young, Henry (c. 1710 - 1752), and William. Their five daughters were Sarah, who married William Hathaway (1695 - 1772); Ann, who died unmarried in 1761; Margaret;

Typical household items that are listed in Lawson inventories.

Elizabeth, who married Robert Biscoe in 1727; and Judith, who married Francis Timberlake in 1730.[14]

The size of Henry Lawson's family illustrates the difficulty faced by a successful small planter family with its gentry background in England in maintaining such a status in Christ Church Parish. While a holding of 375 acres could place Henry Lawson near the top among small planters in Lancaster County, it could not guarantee a successful future for his children. Henry and Mary Lawson separated out the 125 acres that had come to her from her mother, Elizabeth Baker, and entailed it, meaning they specified who could inherit the land. The entailment went to Epaphroditus Lawson, trustee for Rowland Lawson, and his heirs, to Mary Lawson for her use during her natural life, then to Rowland, son of Henry and Mary Lawson and his male heirs, and lacking them, to John Kelly, son of Mary Sallard Kelly Lawson and her first husband, and to Henry Lawson, son of Mary and Henry Lawson and his heirs, and finally to other heirs of Henry and Mary Lawson.[15] Henry and Mary at the same time made an entailed deed of gift for 125 acres, the upper end of the 250-acre portion of their land, to John Kelly, Mary's son by her first marriage and his male heirs, and lacking them to Rowland Lawson, son of Henry and Mary, and his male heirs, lacking them to Henry Lawson, son of Henry and Mary, and his male heirs, and then to the other heirs of Henry and Mary (the daughters.)[16] When Henry Lawson died in 1725, he left no will. He had eight tithables in 1720. Perhaps the terms of any servants had already expired, so that there were no indentures or slaves to leave to his heirs.

The third Rowland Lawson, who had inherited a larger portion of the lands of their father, Rowland, than had his brother Henry, married Jane (or Jean) Glasscock. They became the parents of seven children. Their sons were Rowland (4), Thomas, John, and Anthony, and their daughters were Joanna, Sarah, and Elizabeth. When Rowland (3) wrote his will in November 1716, all these children were still living. His widow, Jane, was to have use of one-third of the house and plantation on which they lived during her life and the same share of the other three plantations. Rowland (4) was his principal heir, and in addition to the bequest of "my still and my gunn" was to inherit all the land and tenements for himself and his male heirs. Lacking such, the land was to go in the same way to each of the sons. Another third of the other three plantations was to be used for the education of the two minor sons, John and Anthony. The remainder of the estate — personal property, slaves, livestock — was to be appraised and divided into eighths, with one-eighth going to each of the seven children and the widow, with his nephew, Rowland Lawson, son of Henry, to receive one young cow when he reached 18.[17]

It was the fate of Thomas Lawson to inherit all the land. He was the only surviving brother among the four. With 900 acres in Christ Church Parish, he became the most successful of the large family of Lawson cousins clustered in the parish. In October 1734 he sold 100 acres to John Steptoe, leaving him with 800 acres. Although Thomas cared carefully for his inherited lands, he did sell two parcels. In 1733 he sold one parcel of 25 acres known as the Broken Islands at the mouth of Mosquito Creek to George Turberville for £21 current Virginia money. In 1734 a parcel of 100 acres was sold to John Steptoe.[18]

The Steptoe sale is interesting, for its deed offers a picture of the community of landholdings that belonged to the Lawson kinship circle in the area around the present community of White Stone.

Although the various branches of the Lawson family seem to have lived amicably near each other for the most part, occasional friction arose. One occasion was in April 1740 when Johanna Lawson Steptoe and her husband John Steptoe, Jr., sued her brother, Thomas Lawson, executor of the estate of their mother, Jane Glasscock Lawson, widow and surviving executor of Roland Lawson (3), over distribution of the estate. Johanna Steptoe's one-third share of her father's estate was to be £615.13.8. Thomas Lawson was to receive the same amount and their mother the other third. When the suit was finally settled in October 1740, the court found for John and Johanna Steptoe, ordering Thomas to pay them £17.7.9 and 3 farthings.[19]

When Thomas Lawson died in 1747, the court appointed three neighbors, Abraham Currell, Nicholas Martin, and William Dymer, to take an inventory of his possessions, as the law of the colony required. Few other documents are so revealing of the material quality of life and personal wealth of an individual as an inventory. Thomas Lawson's inventory showed an estate in which the livestock, furniture, tools, and household goods were valued at £165/13/10 ½ and his slaves at £526/03/10 ½.[20]

Among the 14 slaves were four men, George, Tom, Charles, and Harry. George was probably elderly, as his value was low. Of the five women, Nan, Martha, Ester, Sarah, and another Nan, Ester was probably elderly. There were three boys, one girl, and another one simply named Agga, with no gender or value listed. Nine of the 14 would appear to have been able-bodied workers on Lawson's plantation.

His livestock included four cows with calves, a large bull, five barren cows, seven young heifers, four yearling steers, three sows, 13 piglets, nine young hogs, 12 shoats, a

A trunk and a tea kettle were among the items in Thomas Lawson's estate inventory.

ewe, and a lamb. The quantity of livestock suggests that Lawson not only raised enough to feed his family and slaves, but also to market some.

Thomas Lawson had a mare and colt, a young horse, a sorrel horse, and a white horse, the latter two more than twice as valuable as the other three. The two saddles suggest that the sorrel and the white were both riding horses. Whether his plow and harrow were drawn by a horse or by an ox cannot be determined. Their presence indicates Lawson probably engaged in growing grain as well as tobacco and practiced a more sophisticated form of farming than spade cultivation tobacco, which was the most typical agricultural practice in Lancaster County's first century.

Lawson's furniture was indicative of the living standard of a comfortable small planter of the mid-18th century. The two large oval tables and a dozen walnut chairs that were fashionable in the second quarter of the century would permit seating of the family and several guests for dinners. The half dozen tea cups with "dishes," most likely cups without handles but with deep saucers, a tea kettle, and "sundries tea ware" enabled the Lawsons to entertain those guests according to the style of the times for gentry in the Anglo-American world. Lawson's possession of "1 set of silver shoe and knee buckles" as well as a gold ring and a watch reveal his eye for fashionable display.

In addition to the fashionable consumption of tea, other beverages in which the Lawsons partook included hard cider, for the inventory listed 14 old cider casks, two mugs, and a black jack, which was a leather tankard for beer or cider. Three wineglasses would indicate consumption of another beverage favored by planters, and a coffee mill and coffeepot show that this drink, gaining in popularity in the colonies, was a part of the Lawson household diet. Lawson's two flasks, a punch bowl, and two stills suggest manufacture and use of stronger spirits than cider or wine, perhaps brandy or whiskey. One still, valued at £10, was the second most valuable individual item in the inventory, behind only the best bed in the house, valued at £14/1/0.

The Lawsons seem to have eaten on treenware — wooden trenchers — or on pewter, for aside from "an old parcel of earthenware," the teacups give the only hint of chinaware. The pewter is hard to determine, for it was weighed in the inventory at 93 pounds. Whether this was usable hollowware and plates or broken pieces to be melted down or sold cannot be determined. Lawson had a spoon mold, indicating that he may have made pewter spoons there for the household. Two brass candlesticks would seem to be the nicest decorative objects in the house. The large number of tablecloths, 10, of which four were diaper (a diamond-pattern cloth) listed individually by value, tell us that his table was customarily covered at mealtime. There were, however, only six napkins in the house.

Some indication of the size and design of Thomas Lawson's house emerges from the naming of the rooms in the inventory. These were the closet (usually a small bedroom), the chamber (a bedroom), the hall (a large room that combined the functions of a living room and dining room) and a hall chamber (a bedroom either adjacent to, or above, the hall). These four rooms suggest a story-and-a half house, with two rooms down and two up, typical of the lifestyle and architecture of middling Virginia planters in the first half of the 18th century.

The actual furniture in the house was adequate but not exceptional. The two oval tables and the dozen walnut chairs were the principal furnishings of the hall, the gathering place for the household and for guests. The seven leather chairs were probably older oak chairs upholstered in leather seats and backs that had possibly been dining chairs in the home of Thomas' parents, but by the time of Lawson's death had been scattered to other rooms. One old desk appeared on the inventory just after the list of books, suggesting that the books may have been stored in it. Only one chest of drawers is men-

tioned, indicating that most storage of textiles and clothing took place in the four leather trunks and two chests, which were probably located in the two bedrooms upstairs.

The most valuable objects in the house were the three beds "& furniture," a phrase indicating that they were complete with roping, ticking stuffed with flock, a mat that fit between the rope and the tick, and a set of curtains and valances for privacy and protection from drafts. A fourth bed was without curtains. The beds were located in the closet, the chamber, and the hall chamber. For each bed there was a chamber pot and the house also contained a close stool, a chair that was a toilet. An oval table, a square table, and two looking glasses completed the furniture in Thomas Lawson's house.

His items for food preparation included a tin pot, some brass spoons, two sifters, an iron pot, two milk

pans, six butter pots, three frying pans, a bell metal skillet, an old kettle, a mortar and pestle, and several tubs and pans. The presence of only one shovel and tongs suggests a single fireplace in the house, probably located in the hall. This could have been used for cooking as well as for warmth, or there may have been a kitchen outbuilding.

Thomas Lawson's tools comprised only the basic necessities. They included a parcel of carpenter's tools, an auger, a penknife, sheep shears, two pairs of scissors, a small axe, a grindstone, a gardener's knife, fleams, a claw hammer, a parcel of shoemaker's tools, cotton cards, and a branding iron. The household had a spinning wheel, indicating that the women were making yarn or thread.

Thomas Lawson's library offers considerable insight into the man and his interests. It was not large, but its principal focus reveals a man of sincere piety and attachment to his church. He had an Old Testament, a New Testament, and four prayer books. This suggests that he and his family could bring the prayer books to Christ Church on Sundays to follow the service and that the family also may have gathered at home for the reading of Morning or Evening Prayer. In addition, he had a copy of *The Whole Duty of Man*, a highly popular book of Anglican piety, a book of sermons, and "a parcel of old books," unfortunately with no authors or titles listed. Only two other books are mentioned by name, "1 books mercts.," and "1 book of cookery." The merchant's book was most likely *The Merchant's Magazine, or Factors Guide,* the book compiled and published by Lawson's Lancaster county neighbor and kinsman, Robert Biscoe. Biscoe was married to Elizabeth Lawson, daughter of Henry Lawson. As a neighbor of Thomas Lawson, Biscoe was witness to a lease for his kinsman.[21] The cookery book indicates that Mrs. Lawson was an educated woman who could read and who had an interest in careful and varied food preparation for her family.

Thomas Lawson seemed in need of cash on a regular basis, possibly because he was usually in debt. Whether this was the result of poor money management on his part, a perennially depressed tobacco market, or destructive habits such as living extravagantly and gambling, cannot be ascertained from surviving documents. One method of acquiring needed cash was to rent his land. His lease in July 1742 of 100 acres to George Currell, who already owned a neighboring plantation, promised to yield him 850 pounds of tobacco annually plus an allowance for cask.[22] He rented another 100 acres to Robert Biscoe and provided in his will that when this lease expired, the land was to be sold to pay his debts and for the benefit of his son. He was indebted to his brother-in-law, John Steptoe, who had married Lawson's sister Johanna, for £43 sterling, for which he sold him 100 acres of land in 1734.[23]

The debts were substantial, for Lawson's will, written on July 14, 1747, provided that five of the slaves be sold to pay the debts and that his executors sell timber from his land for the same purpose and for the benefit of his son.[24] Lawson had died by August 14, 1747, when his will was admitted to probate. That was the same day the inventory was admitted. Thomas and Margaret Lawson had only one surviving child, a son, Thomas. Whether there had been other children is not known. It was perhaps fortunate that this was so, for Thomas passed on a smaller estate from the one he had inherited from his own father, thanks to the early deaths of his brothers.

Henry Lawson, Jr., cousin and contemporary of Thomas Lawson, was a leading citizen of Lancaster. It was his sister, Elizabeth, who had married Robert Biscoe in 1727, and it was they who rented land from Thomas Lawson. His sister Sarah married William Hathaway by 1732, and his sister Judith married Francis Timberlake in 1730. Henry was the son of Henry Lawson, Sr., who died in 1725, and his wife Mary Sallard Kelly Lawson. The wife of Henry, Jr., was Winifred, whose maiden name is not known.[25]

Henry, Jr., and Winifred had several children, but they are not named in his will. They were probably Henry, who died in 1755, just three years after his father; William, who lived until

1789 and married Betty Sydnor; Mary, who married John Riveer; Elizabeth, who died unmarried in 1771; and Ann.[26]

Henry Lawson did not appear to live on as gracious a scale as his cousin Thomas. His landholdings amounted to 250 acres in the rent rolls of 1748 and 1750. He may have been a successful agriculturalist, as the 1746 rent roll indicated he had a significant workforce of seven slaves for his acreage: Will, Tom, Daniel, George, Phillis, Janey, and Hannah. His inventory mentioned another slave, Judith. At £69, the value of his personal property was quite modest, less than half that of his cousin Thomas Lawson's estate.

Yet it was Henry, not Thomas, who was selected for two of the most important local government positions, justice and vestryman. Henry was named a justice of the Lancaster County Court in 1731, 1735, 1738, but in 1742 he refused to serve and asked to be left off the list. He had also been chosen for the vestry by 1736.[27]

The descendants of another Lawson managed to hold their own for three generations. When Epaphroditus (2) died in 1722, he left a lengthy inventory that included 13 slaves and indicated a five-room, story-and-a-half house. He bequeathed an annual income to his sister to care for his children, Epaphroditus (3), called Eppa; Nicholas, who died in 1750; and Judith. When they came of age, the three were to inherit equal shares of their father's estate, which included 200 acres.[28] When Epaphroditus (3) died in 1745, his estate was valued at £350, including his nine slaves. He left two sons, Epaphroditus (4) and John. Each of these boys was to be apprenticed, Epaphroditus to David Galloway & Geo. Ker & Co., Northumberland, Merchants, and John "after his schooling, was to be bound to a trade at age 16 to serve until he was 20."[29] These young men would not be able to count on sufficient income from land and the labor of slaves to support them, and would have to earn a living working in trade or a craft.[30]

The Lawson family represents stability and continuity in the life of colonial Christ Church Parish. In the early years they generously shared their land, and family cohesiveness is shown in the continued use of family names across generations and lines of kinship. By 1750 they had resided in the parish and on the same land for a century. The division of the early large land grants in the White Stone area into smaller plantations for subsequent generations, coupled with the failure to acquire large additional holdings, left power, on a level beyond the county and parish, as well as real wealth, beyond their grasp. Still, the Lawsons and the friends and neighboring families with which they were allied by marriage, including Biscoe, Currell, Hathaway, and Steptoe, formed a tight-knit community whose members looked out for each other.

ENDNOTES

[1]Nell Marion Nugent, *Cavaliers and Pioneers: Abstracts of Virginia Land Patents and Grants, 1623-1800,* Volume I (Richmond: Press of the Dietz Printing Co., 1934) shows at least 10 land transactions in the Isle of Wight County and Upper Norfolk County between 1635 and 1643 in which Epaphroditus Lawson acquired land. I:35, 53, 74-75, 84, 106, 135, 151.
[2]Ibid., 135.
[3]FHCCRF - Parish Profile Archives. For information on Elizabeth Lawson Davis, only child of the first Epaphroditus, the immigrant, see W.G. Stanard, "Abstracts of Virginia Land Patents," *Virginia Magazine of History and Biography*, 4 (1897), 313.
[4]Nugent, *Cavaliers and Pioneers*, I, 217.
[5]Ibid., 297.
[6]W.G. Stanard, "Abstracts of Virginia Land Patents," VMHB 4 (1897), 313.
[7]Lancaster County Deed Book 4:60, 322.
[8]Lancaster County Will Book 10:415.
[9]Gertrude E. Gray, *Virginia Northern Neck Land Grants, 1694-1742* (Baltimore: Genealogical Publishing Co., Inc., 1988), 2-303, 22.
[10]Rowland Lawson will written 4 March 1704/05, probated 11 September 1706. Lancaster County Will Book 8:136.
[11]W.G. Stanard, "Abstracts of Virginia Land Patents," *VMHB* 4 (1897): 313.
[12]Lancaster County Deed Book 9:387.
[13]See Henry Lawson, Sr., file, Parish Profile Archive.
[14]Ibid. Robert Biscoe, well-educated at London's Christ Hospital, had come to Lancaster County as a bookkeeper indentured to Robert Carter and is the subject of his own biographical sketch in this volume.
[15]Henry Lawson and Mary, his wife, to Epaphroditus Lawson, trustee for Rowland Lawson. Deed of Trust, 12 September 1720, Lancaster County Will Book 11:163-164.
[16]Henry Lawson and Mary Lawson to John Kelly. Entailed deed of gift. 12 September 1720. Lancaster County Will Book 11:162-163
[17]Rowland Lawson will written 23 November 1716, probated 9 January 1717.

Lancaster County Deed and Will Book 10:189. Witnesses were John Turberville, William Sydnor, and Epa Lawson. The executors were his wife, Jane Lawson, son Rowland, and Charles Barber[?].

[18]Lancaster County Deed and Will Book 12:320.

[19]John Steptoe, Jr., and Johanna his wife v. Thomas Lawson. 21 April 1740, 11 July 1740. Lancaster Deed and Will Book 13: 173; Lancaster County Court Order Book, 10 October 1740, 8: 295.

[20]Lancaster County Deed and Will Book 14:152.

[21]When Thomas Lawson rented 100 acres of his land to George Currell, one of the witnesses to the lease was Robert Biscoe. Thomas Lawson to George Currell, 5 July 1742. Lancaster County Will Book 13:282.

[22]Ibid.

[23]Thomas Lawson to John Stepto, 1734. Lancaster County Deed and Will Book 12:320-321.

[24]Lancaster County Will Book 14:147.

[25]Henry Lawon will and inventory, Lancaster County Will Book 15:96, 103.

[26]FHCCRF, Parish Profile Archives, Henry Lawson, Jr., file.

[27]Ibid.

[28]Epaphroditus Lawson will and inventory, 12 December 1722. Lancaster County Will Book 10:408. The 1721 Rent Roll indicated that he owned 200 acres.

[29]Epaphroditus Lawson will, 1745. Lancaster County Will Book 14:179.

[30]Apprenticeship agreement, Epaphroditus Lawson, 11 March 1747. Lancaster County Will Book 14:179.

Robert Anderson, Tailor

No matter where one lived in the mid-18th century, whether a booming city like London or a more remote region like colonial Lancaster County, and no matter what one's level in society, all depended on the skilled hands of the tailor to put clothes on their backs. In that time, there was no ready-made clothing. The outer garments of everyone, from slaves to aristocrats, were tailor-made.

The tailors' trade was the single largest trade in any settled area. Although there were larger numbers of tailors in the bigger cities than in more rural areas, the fact that everyone relied on tailors meant that there was plenty of work. The down side to this scenario was that there was usually a glut of tailors on the work scene. Consequently, tailors rarely made much money and many spent their whole lives as servants. Unlike many other trades with flexible apprenticeship terms, the situation of the tailoring trade necessitated an inflexible length of apprenticeship. The training period for tailors was always a full seven years to make sure that apprentices were sincere in their pursuit of the trade.[1]

Although there were more than a few tailors in Christ Church parish in the first half of the 18th century, the life of one, Robert Anderson, can be pieced together from several bits of documentary evidence. Anderson first appeared in the record books as an indentured servant, but he departed the scene 15 years later as a successful businessman.

Anderson's initial entry in the public records came in 1732 when he is listed in Robert Carter's estate inventory. Anderson was one of a group of 17 white indentured servants living at Carter's home plantation. Among the skilled tradesmen of the group were several carpenters, a gardener, a glazier, a blacksmith, two sailors, two bricklayers, a cook, and two tailors, Robert Anderson and John Conner.[2]

More than likely Anderson and Conner had served full

seven-year apprenticeships in the Old World, and were recruited by Carter's agents for service in Virginia. This meant that they were at least in their mid-twenties at the time of Robert Carter's death. Their situation on the home plantation insured them of constant work, a security that not all tailors could claim. Their presence at Corotoman, however, did not mean that they enjoyed the privilege of making fitted clothes for one of the richest and most powerful men in North America. Quite the contrary, for their jobs probably consisted mainly of making clothing for the numerous slaves and servants under Carter's care. Work on the Carter family's clothing would have been more menial and would have included mending and repair tasks. A man of Carter's stature had enough fashion sense to wear clothing made by the best tailors in London.[3] Evidence of this can be seen in a 1729 letter from Carter to James Bradley in England in which he ordered a number of items including a suit: "And a fashionable suit of broad cloth cloths for my self for the winter, of a grave colour, lined with Shaloon. Mr. How has my measure and knows how to fit me; he took it in Virginia and hath also made me cloaths since I am become much smaller in bulk than I was at that time."[4] Despite being relegated to making clothes for those in the lower stations of parish life, however, Carter's two tailors had steady work and dry goods of almost unlimited variety with which to work. Carter's inventory contains hundreds of yards of cloth from linen to osnaberg to kersey and Holland.[5]

For whatever reason, Anderson was more successful than most members of his trade. At some point after Carter's 1732 death, he branched out on his own. There is strong evidence that he opened his own shop, more than likely as a single room in his own home, but still on an independent level many tailors never achieved. Although this occurred sometime between 1732 and 1741, the exact date remains a mystery because the expiration date of his indenture to Robert Carter is not known.[6]

By the spring of 1741, however, Anderson had achieved the status of master tailor. In May of that year he apprenticed

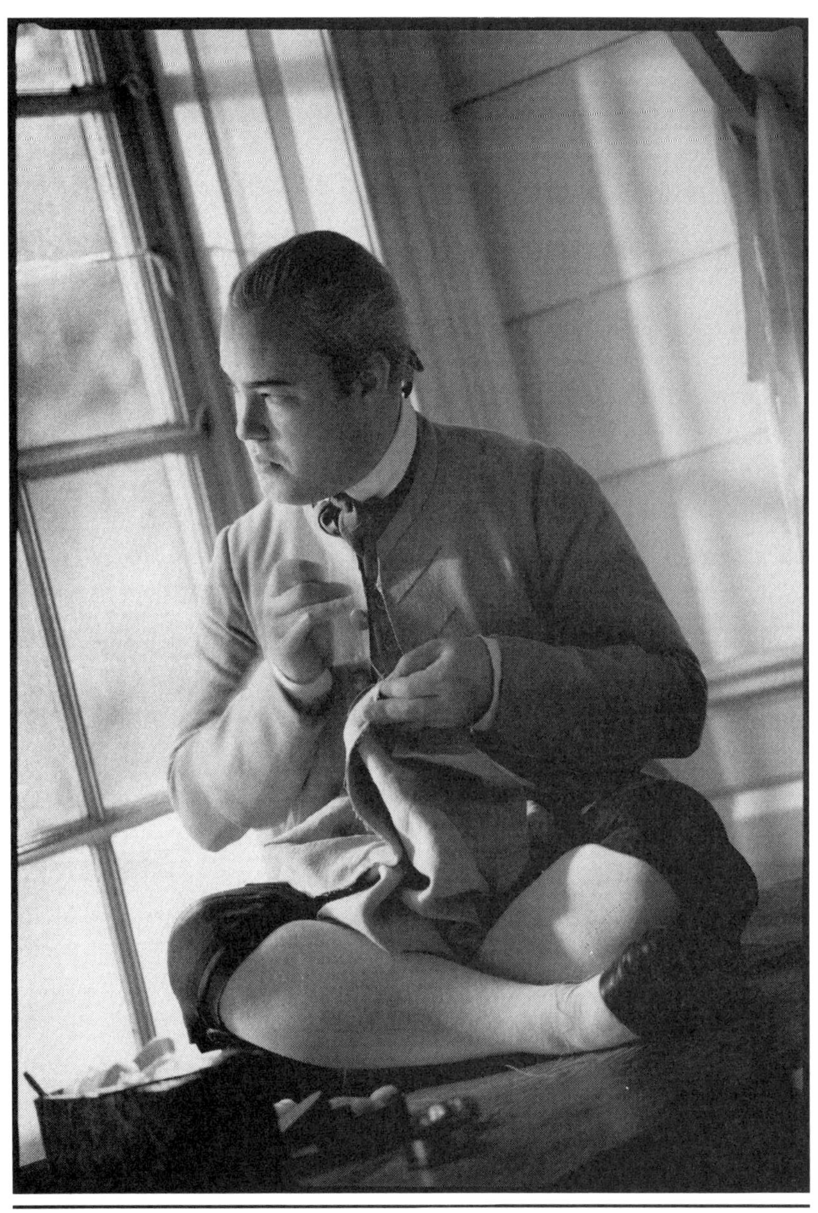

A costumed interpreter at Colonial Williamsburg carries out the tasks of an 18th-century Virginia tailor. Tailors typically sewed while sitting cross-legged in a window for light. (Courtesy Colonial Williamsburg Foundation)

William Carter, the 16-year-old orphan of William Carter. The apprentice was to serve seven years under Anderson during which time Anderson was to teach him "to read and write and the Trade of a Taylor and to find and provide him with sufficient and cleanly dyet lodging and apparell during his service and at the expiration thereof to pay him as is appointed for Servants by Indenture or custom."[7]

During the next several years, Anderson continued to establish himself as a prospering businessman. At some point, he also wed, to a woman named Mary whose surname is not known. There is no evidence that the couple had any children. Anderson eventually located in Precinct A of the parish near Captain James Gordon's quarter plantation and close to the east side of the Christ Church Glebe. In December 1746, he leased a 100-acre tract of land known as Motley's plantation from Ezekiel Gilbert.[8] The lease was for 31 years at the cost of £31 current money. That sum was to be paid in six equal yearly payments, and the lease could be extended for two more terms with the same agreements. In addition, Anderson was to give Gilbert "one ear of corn...at the feast of the birth of our Lord God....and agrees that at the expiration of the term to leave and yield the premises in as good repair as he now finds them." The lease was witnessed by Robert Biscoe, another servant formerly indentured to Carter; James Kirk, a neighboring landholder; and William Carter, possibly Anderson's own apprentice who would have reached the legal age of 21 by 1746.[9]

What we will never know from the handful of public records in which Anderson is mentioned are the details of his life as a tailor. However, careful study of the tailor trade by historians at Colonial Williamsburg can provide some enlightenment into commonalties among all tailors. Although the demand for clothing in the 18th century was unrelenting, it was not the tailor who got rich by providing this necessity of life. Rather, the merchant who sold the cloth to the customer was the one reaping the financial rewards. With the exception of wealthy merchant tailors who had expansive shops and large stocks of dry goods, tailors did not provide the cloth to the customer. Rather, the customer purchased the cloth from a storehouse or directly from a local weaver and then brought it to the tailor. Despite the dozens and dozens of cloth varieties that ranged from drugget to diaper to twill, the average person of the 18th century was much more aware of subtleties of quality and style in dry goods than today's modern customer, not only because nearly everyone was involved in the purchase of cloth but because this was a society filled with active textile makers.

The usual procedure in the process of procuring clothing was that a customer purchased the cloth and took it to the tailor where a fitted garment, such as a gown for a lady or a jacket, a shirt, or breeches for a man, was commissioned. In his 1751 *L'Encyclopédie ou Dictionnaire Raisonné des Sciences, des Arts et des Métiers* Frenchman Denis Diderot described the transaction: "In the tailor shop…the tailor himself measures the client while his men cut, heat the flatirons, and sew by the light of the window, all cross-legged on their counter."[10]

As Diderot intimates, the skill of a tailor lay not in his sewing ability, but in his cutting ability. Nearly everyone in the 18th century could sew, but that simple stitching was confined to household mending or making table linen like napkins or other household items such as sacks or curtains to go on a bed. It took a certain skill to use a pattern and create a garment with sleeves and legs that would comfortably and fashionably fit a person.

Once Anderson or any other tailor had measured the customer, then the material was cut out and sewed together by the tailor as he sat cross-legged on his work board. Artists of the time almost always depict tailors either as standing up with measuring tapes around their necks and shears (scissors) in their hands or sitting cross-legged in a window sewing a garment.

The cross-legged tailor sitting on his board in a window is often humorously referred to as a tailor monkey. This standard image of a tailor is so ancient that the original purpose behind the pose has been lost although the practice, unique to the tailoring trade, has some very practical underpinnings. The cross-legged position is comfortable and useful to the tailor and gives him room to spread out the work project, something that is not easily done in a chair. Sitting in a window supplied lighting for the demands of precise stitching, and, in more urban areas, doubled as an ongoing advertisement for passersby who might be considering commissioning a garment. In a rural area such as the one where Anderson operated his shop, there is little likelihood that Anderson received much advertising benefit from sitting in a window, but he still would have sewn there because of the lighting. Although no particular costume is associated with the trade, tailors are often depicted with their breeches untied at the knees and slippers on their feet – both concessions to comfort while sitting cross-legged for long periods of time.[11]

Anderson's daily business of running a tailor shop caused his name to make its way into the public record on occasion. He made a flurry of appearances in the public records in the 1740s. In October 1741 he was the defendant in a suit with Thomas Harris which was dismissed when neither party appeared in court.[12] Earlier that year he successfully brought suit against William Gibson over a bill whereupon Gibson was ordered to pay Anderson £2.5.9.[13] Anderson did not shy away from using the court system to retrieve what he felt was owed him. A similar suit in 1745 resulted in Lawrence Blade being ordered to pay Anderson £1.10.0 and 500 pounds of tobacco which he owed by "obligation." In 1746 Anderson pursued the estate of John Taylor for a debt of just over £4 which he received. Also in 1746 he went to court to claim goods of his that got caught up in legal maneuverings between David Galloway, merchant, and James Donallen. Under oath Anderson claimed to own a tester bed[14] with its accompanying accouterments including curtains to be pulled around the bed. He also claimed four head of cattle, a large iron pot, and a rack. The court apparently found for Anderson and ordered the items delivered to him by the Lancaster sheriff. Anderson kept a steady supply of labor at hand. In the 1746 tithable list, Anderson is responsible for the levy of two tithables, himself and John Jones. In August 1747, he acquired the labor of Sarah Smith in an interesting court case that leaves modern readers wondering about the surrounding circumstances. In August of that year Smith came into court and volunteered to serve Anderson for six years. In return he agreed to pay Smith's fine for misbehaving at an earlier court hearing of Elizabeth Pridmore. Anderson also consented to allowing Smith's child to remain with her under his care at no cost to the parish. When her six-year indenture concluded, Smith was to get 30 shillings from Anderson in lieu of the standard freedom dues.[15]

Anderson died shortly after that, and Smith appeared in the estate inventory with six years left on her contract at a value of £5. Also listed in the inventory was Matthew McDaniel, who had three years to serve on an indenture, and "1 negro woman and her child," who were slaves.

Anderson's death in September 1747 leaves historians with one final glimpse into the life of this 18th-century tradesman. Valued at just over £95, his estate afforded him a more comfortable living than most tailors for the time period, but not a lavish one. Of that amount, £34 was in indentures or slaves, labor which was used in either his shop or on the farm. What was being produced on the 100-acre plantation is not known except for the 17 swine, 11 cattle, and five sheep that were listed in the inventory. There was also a plow but no other cultivation tools like hoes, rakes, or sickles. Anderson was apparently literate, as he had a "parcel of old books," and he was able to afford a few luxuries such as a looking glass, window glass, and a pair of silver shoe buckles. He had three guns, one of which was new, and a riding horse as well as a saddle and bridle. There are some indications of wool and cotton production taking place in the household with a wool wheel and cards and both spun and unspun cotton on the inventory list. There were several pieces of leather

and some more being tanned. There were also medical items including vials, gallepots, and lancets.[16]

In actuality, one has to look closely at the inventory to realize that Anderson was a tailor. There is "1 old box iron & heeters," which is a type of iron used to press finished garments or large pieces of cloth. There is also "1 goos" and "3

pr. shears." The shears are tailoring scissors, while the goose is a long narrow iron used for pressing seams during the construction of garments. Mysteriously missing from the inventory are his work board and thimbles.[17]

Anderson appears in the Lancaster records twice more. His wife, Mary, was administrator of his estate. She did not remain a widow long. Before April 1749 she had married Cornelius Mullen. In September 1748, Mullen picked up the lease on Motley's Plantation in lieu of a debt owed him by Ezekiel Gilbert, the owner of the plantation who had leased it to Anderson for 31 years. This time the terms were for 21 years and £35 Virginia money.[18] The following spring, April 1749, "Cornelius Mullen and Mary his wife, adm. of Robert Anderson, dec'd" took Peter Lee to court and won a settlement of £1.11.1/2.[19]

With that final entry in the Lancaster order book, Robert Anderson passed out of local memory, but by piecing together his story we can get a better idea of the life of one middle class, landless tradesman who lived in Christ Church Parish, ran a business there, and died there.

Endnotes

[1]Interview with Mark Hutter, master tailor, Colonial Williamsburg, February 2001.

[2]Robert Carter's inventory, 1732, p. 12. Typed transcript in FHCCRF, original at Alderman Library, University of Virginia.

[3]Hutter interview.

[4]Robert Carter to James Bradley, 26 August 1729, Robert Carter letterbook #3 (August 1728-July 1731), letter 52, University of Virginia.

[5]Carter inventory. It is hard to distinguish which dry goods were meant for sale and which were for use in clothing the servants and slaves on the Carter plantations.

[6]The reason that Anderson appears in the inventory is because he has some time left on his indenture, or contract, with Carter. This meant that there was a monetary value to his labor that must be included in the inventory. Anderson's indenture would still have to be fulfilled despite Carter's death.

[7]Lancaster County Court Order Book, 1729-1743, 8 May 1741, 310.

[8]Motley's Plantation has an interesting history. In 1701 Ruth Wright granted the land to a black woman named Motley for the rest of her life. The 100-acre tract of land apparently retained the name "Motley's Plantation" long after Motley's death.

[9]Lancaster County Deed and Will Book 14:198.

[10]Denis Diderot, *"L'Encyclopédie ou Dictionnaire Raisonné des Sciences, des Arts et des Métiers"* (Originally printed in 1751, reprinted as *A Diderot Pictorial Encyclopedia of Trades and Industry, Manufactures and the Technical Arts in Plates*, vol. II, edited with an introduction and notes by Charles C. Gillispie, Dover Publications, 1987), Plate 440.

[11]Hutter interview.

[12]Lancaster County Court Order Book, 1729-1743, 9 October 1741, 325.

[13]Ibid., 12 June 1741, 316. Interestingly enough, Gibson owned Motley's Plantation which Anderson eventually leased from William Gibson's brother-in-law, Ezekiel Gilbert.

[14]A four-poster bed.

[15]Lancaster County Court Order Book 9, 13 September 1745, 79; 11 April 1746, 95; 12 December 1746, 117.

[16]The vials were to hold medicines, the gallepots were for various ointments and salves, and lancets were used to open wounds or to draw blood.

[17]Lancaster Deed and Will Book 14:161-163.

[18]Lancaster Deed and Will Book 14:213.

[19]There is no known connection between this Lee and any of the more prominent Lee family members of Westmoreland County or to any other Lee families of the area. Lancaster County Court Order Book 9, 14 April 1749, 183.

THOMAS EDWARDS, GENTLEMAN CLERK OF THE COURT

Throughout the colonial period, Lancaster County was an agrarian society. The acquisition of land and its successful cultivation ensured minimally the survival of its inhabitants and optimally a profitable enterprise. The successful landholder was able to purchase additional acreage as well as the labor of white indentured servants or slaves of African descent to work on it.

Land passed from one individual to another by deed, gift, or will. Colonial law mandated that each transaction be recorded, and it assigned that responsibility to the clerk of the county. The clerk's duties and, concomitantly, his fees as established by the General Assembly of the colony, are included in a listing of over 70 specific items in the laws of Virginia.[1] On May 8, 1721, Alexander Spotswood, Lt. Governor and Commander in Chief of the Colony of Virginia, commissioned Thomas Edwards to serve as Clerk of the County of Lancaster.[2]

Edwards, born January 29, 1695, was the son of a prominent Gloucester County physician, Richard Edwards, and his first wife, Mary, who died 20 days after the birth of twins. Thomas was 12 years old when his mother died. Dr. Edwards married secondly, Joanna, mother of several children including John Edwards, whose story appears briefly but dramatically later in this account.[3] Although surviving records reveal nothing about his education, Thomas seems to have been schooled in law, a decided advantage in his position even though the law prohibited him from practicing his profession while serving as clerk.

With a secure income assured him as clerk, on August 4, 1722, Thomas married Sarah Ingram Swan, widow of John Swan and the mother of two little girls, Judith and Ann.[4] Sarah's dower was the easternmost 200 acres on Fleets Bay Neck, which the late John Swan had inherited from his father, Alexander, in 1709.[5]

As was the custom in English common law, that plantation on Fleets Bay Neck became the property of Thomas Edwards upon Sarah's marriage to him and here he established his office.[6] This location was more convenient for conducting the business of the people in the eastern precincts of the county than the courthouse and clerk's facility at Corotoman on the western side of the Western Branch of the Corrotoman River.[7]

Shortly after his marriage, Edwards found himself in the unenviable position of being the plaintiff in a lawsuit against Col. Robert Carter, the richest and most powerful man in the county. The late John Swan, first husband of Edwards' wife, had had a dissentious relationship with his step-mother, Alexander Swan's widow, Mary, over the division of the elder Swan's estate. A controversial and bitter lawsuit ensued.[8] Mary Swan was the elder sister of Robert Carter's second wife, Betty, and when Mary died, Carter was appointed administrator of her estate.[9] Apparently the animosity engendered between the principals endured and was perpetuated long after John's and Mary's deaths. Edwards, on his wife's behalf, brought suit against Carter protesting the amount of money that Carter had spent for Mary Swan's funeral.[10]

Carter was privately critical of the new clerk at the time of that case, referring to him as "a little petty fogging lawyer."[11] Regardless of Carter's judgment, Edwards seems to have carried out the duties of his office to almost everyone's satisfaction. As time passed, Carter and Edwards came to terms with their differences, maintaining, as one would expect of men of their standing in the community, a reasonable degree of civility and eventually a social relationship.[12]

Unquestionably, Edwards attained prominence and earned respect in the county and in the parish. He was capable and conscientious, and in some way or at some time, he touched the life of every person in the community. He issued marriage licenses, probated wills, and recorded inventories. For preparing certificates and bonds his fee was 50 pounds of tobacco. He attended orphan's courts and entered guardian accounts. He entered the records of deeds and issued orders for appointing constables and grand juries. He entered the levy (tax assessment) and made a copy thereof. For the innumerable copies he made, his lawful fee was one pound of tobacco for every 30 words. One pound of tobacco was worth slightly less than one penny.[13]

There were dozens of other responsibilities for the clerk of a colonial Virginia county, including swearing of witnesses at a trial, administering oaths, and recording verdicts and depositions. Many of these duties required Edwards to make the considerable journey to the courthouse, where he also had some office space. Certainly he was present at criminal trials and hearings before the justices, but he spent much of his time in his 'home office' on Fleets Bay Neck. Fleets Bay Road was laid out and surveyed by the early 18th century and was often designated as a boundary in deeds.[14]

Their daily routines and responsibilities occupied most of Thomas and Sarah's time, but all else would be set aside on Sunday as the family joined its neighbors to worship at Christ Church. This, with its counterpart, St. Mary's White Chapel in the northwestern sector of the county, was the focal point of the community. The parishioners took their devotions seriously, following the long-established rites of the Church of England.[15] At Christ Church all the people of the parish gathered to worship, but the women such as Sarah Edwards and their children especially must have anticipated the sociability afforded by meeting before and after worship with neighbors and friends they saw only at church. In the 1730s the people of the parish watched with interest as a beautiful new brick church was being built. About the time the church was completed in 1735, Edwards was one of 12 men appointed to the vestry. In 1737, Edwards and John Carter, son of Col. Robert Carter, were selected as church wardens.[16]

Lancaster County was a close-knit community and the people were probably aware of issues of dissension in their ranks. Apparently, the minister, the Reverend John Bell, occasionally used his pulpit to address these issues subtly. Referring in 1723 to the suit brought by Edwards against him, Robert Carter wrote in his diary "... Mr. Bell, in his discourse about Envy, had several plain innuendoes at Thomas Edwards and my differences."[17]

While Edwards attended to his many professional duties, he undoubtedly kept a close watch on the production of his plantation. He and Sarah, who was by no means idle, maintained a large laboring force of slaves and servants to tend the fields, care for the livestock and outbuildings, and help run this busy household.

Four of the six children born to Sarah and Thomas during the first decade of their marriage survived. The birth of Thomas Jr., in 1725, eased the grief of losing their firstborn, John. Their next son, Richard, died in infancy, but soon two daughters, Mary and Sarah, and a son, Robert, followed. Sarah, as mistress of a 200-acre plantation, directed and took part in cooking, sewing, keeping the kitchen garden, and childcare. Judith and Ann Swan, children of her first marriage, were good company for their mother and surely enjoyed playing with and overseeing their young Edwards siblings, children of Thomas, the father they grew up with.[18]

Ann Ingram, Sarah's mother, survived her husband John by 12 years, and when she died in 1733, Sarah and Thomas Edwards inherited her very substantial holdings. Their grandmother Ingram made generous provisions when they reached adulthood for Judith and Ann Swan, Thomas Edwards, Jr., and her other three Edwards grandchildren living at the time she died. (Five more children were born to the couple after Ann Ingram's death.)[19]

A year after the death of her grandmother, Judith Swan married William Heale, who died a year or so after the marriage. Ann Swan married Dr. John Edwards, younger half-brother of her stepfather, Thomas. Judith married secondly, Griffin Fauntleroy. After her daughters had left home to create their own households, Sarah gave birth to Richard in 1735, (the second son so named), and two years later to Elizabeth. Another daughter, Milly, died a month after her birth, but Lucy their youngest daughter, lived to adulthood.[20]

In June 1740, Edwards, as clerk of Lancaster County, "produced in court sundry loose sheets and quires of papers containing the most ancient and valuable Records belonging to this county." Perhaps these were the "Parcel of bundles containing Deeds, Wills Petitions, Declarations" that Catherine Dare, widow of Edwards's predecessor William Dare, clerk from 1716 to 1720, had turned over to Edwards in April 1724. Perhaps they came from another unnamed source. In either case, the court was concerned to preserve the records by transcribing them in a 'proper book.' When Edwards offered to transcribe the records for a payment of 2,000 pounds of tobacco, (which in the estimation of later historians and genealogists, was a priceless endeavor) the court accepted the offer.[21]

Edwards was an accomplished man, and to a great extent, unique in early 18th-century Lancaster society. He was a full-time professional when most of his contemporaries were chiefly concerned with the production of their plantations, their fortunes rising and falling depending upon the vagaries of weather and pestilence. His attendance upon the affairs of the county and the parish seem, in retrospect, to be all consuming, but there was another side to the man, and by careful perusal of the records, it too is revealed. It speaks to his character and his humanity. References are found in neighbors' wills mentioning Thomas Edwards as "my good friend," and "my loving friend." He had a warm and close relationship with Landon Carter, youngest son of Col. Robert Carter.[22] Above and beyond attending to the awesome responsibilities he had undertaken for the betterment of the community at large, Edwards engendered respect and admiration on a personal level with his neighbors.

As in most families, there were events that brought joy, but there were also terrible sorrows. For the Edwards family,

1743 was a year of intense emotions. Ann Swan Edwards and husband, Dr. John Edwards, were probably living then on John's plantation of 1,200 acres in King George County, at the falls of the Rappahannock. Their two children, Richard Swan Edwards and little Sarah were Thomas and Sarah's first grandchildren and probably brought much joy to the family. In March 1743, tragedy struck. Indians purportedly killed Dr. John Edwards on his way to attend a sick patient. His untimely and dreadful death certainly shocked not only the family, but also the community where Ann had grown up. Sarah was expecting her last child during this ordeal, but the baby, born in August, lived only a week.[23] A month later, Thomas Edwards, Jr., took the oath of office of Deputy Clerk of Lancaster County. This afforded the family an opportunity to put their grief behind them and look to the future.[24]

For the next three years, father and son worked together on the business of the county. Thomas Jr., had an exemplary role model to learn from and emulate. By 1746, Thomas was 21, at which time he assumed the full duties of clerk of the county. His parents deeded him properties of 100 and 200 acres inherited from his grandmother, Ann Ingram, as stipulated in her will.[25] It was a joyous time for the Edwards family as they celebrated the weddings of two of their children. Young Thomas married Elizabeth Fauntleroy, and their oldest daughter, Mary, married Major John Fleet, both members of respected landholding county families.[26]

Thomas Jr., petitioned "to move the court for their approbation to his residing and keeping his office at the late dwelling place of Mr. John Eustace which said Thomas intends to purchase in the line between this (Lancaster) and Northumberland Counties." The court agreed that this would be a more convenient place to keep the office and granted Edwards leave to do so.[27] On July 17, 1747, the clerk recorded a deed for 475 acres "lying and being part in Northumberland and part in Lancaster County" that John Eustace,

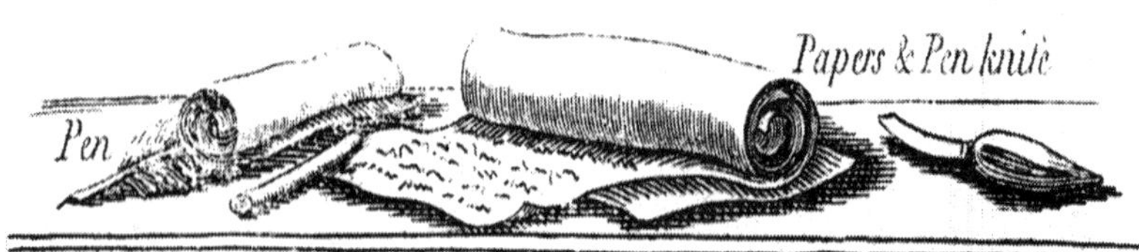

Northumberland County, Wicomico Parish, sold to Thomas Edwards, Jr., Lancaster County, Christ Church Parish.[28]

After 25 years, the Edwards plantation on Fleets Bay Neck, so long a center of county activity, was again just a residence. Thomas Sr., did not fully retire. He served as Prosecutor for the King for several more years and Sarah still had the care of their younger children, but by then middle aged, their lives must have been a little easier. They prospered and marked 35 years together in the home place where they had spent most of their adult years.

Thomas Edwards, Sr., died in 1759, but Sarah lived another 12 years. Her husband had assured her rightful place at her long-time home. His will stated, "with the-consent of my dear and loving wife, I give unto her . . . the sole and uninterrupted use of my dwelling plantation during her natural life."[29] As specified in that will, their youngest son, Richard, inherited the 200 acres on Fleets Bay Neck when Sarah died. Thomas and Robert, Richard's older brothers, had received their inheritances (originally their grandmother Ingram's property), while their parents were still living.[30] In 1771, Richard sold the property to Thomas Rowand and the significant Edwards family presence on Fleets Bay Neck came to an end.

ENDNOTES

[1]William Waller Hening, ed. *The Statutes at Large Being a Collection of the Laws of Virginia* (New York: R. & W. & G. Bartow, 1823), 4:344-348.

[2]Lancaster County Court Order Book 6:342. Edwards succeeded William Dare as clerk of the court. On 10 May 1721, after recording that Edwards took the oath as clerk of the court, the order book shows that Catherine Dare, widow of William Dare, was ordered to deliver to Edwards all records belonging to the court. This she finally did on 8 April 1724, according to the careful list Edwards recorded at that time.

[3]Ruby Lee Edwards, *Doctor Richard Edwards Some of His Descendants and Allied Families* (undated, self-published, photocopied) in collec-

tion of Mary Ball Washington Museum and Library, Lancaster, Va.

[4]Lancaster County Marriage Register,1715-1782.

[5]Will of Alexander Swan, Lancaster County Will Book 10:11.

[6]Christ Church Parish, Lancaster County, Rent Rolls, 1720-1750. Originals housed at the Virginia State Library and Archives in Richmond, Virginia. Photocopies in FHCCRF. The rent rolls list the 200 acres, but the processioners records and the county road surveyors orders pinpointed the location of the land and identified an office as being on the land.

[7]Nina Tracy Mann, researcher and compiler, *Queenstown*, Mary Ball Washington Museum and Library, Lancaster, Va.

[8]Christine Adams Jones, compiler, "Order Book Entries at Lancaster County Courthouse, Lancaster, Virginia, referring to Robert Carter of Corotoman, 1663-1732," 100-101. FHCCRF.

[9]Ibid., 108.

[10]Ibid., 115.

[11]Robert Carter to Landon Jones, 22 July 1723, Robert Carter Letterbook, transcription by Francis Berkeley, 1:63-65. FHCCRF.

[12]Robert Carter Diary 1722-1728, 5 February, 10 March 1723. Transcribed from a partially corrected, typed transcript property of the University of Virginia Library, lent by Francis L. Berkeley, solely for reference and research use by the Historic Christ Church Foundation volunteers.

[13]The Lancaster County Court set the rate of 7½ d (seven and a half pence) or 6 pounds of tobacco, and 6 d. (six pence) or 5 pounds of tobacco. Lancaster County Court Order Book 8:33 (1729-1743, 14 April 1731).

[14]One of the assignments of the Surveyors of Highways included ". . . the highway from Col. Carter's Mill [today known as the Lancaster Roller Mill on Rt. 3], to the place known as Jackson's mill [familiarly Duntons], and to the clerk's office of the County in Christ Church Parish." This is the first known reference to the clerk's office. This assignment was repeated yearly through 1746. After that, the assignment was for Fleets Neck. Lancaster County Court Order Books 7:84 and 9:96, Surveyors of Highways assignments.

[15]For good descriptions of the colonial Virginia church and its leadership structure, see David L. Holmes, *A Brief History of the Episcopal Church* (Valley Forge, Pa,: Trinity Press International, 1993), 20-22; Robert Prichard, *A History of the Episcopal Church*, (Harrisburg, Pa.: Morehouse Publishing, 1991), 8-11; Dell Upton, *Holy Things and Profane: Anglican Parish Churches in Colonial Virginia* (New Haven and London: Yale University Press, 1986), 6-10. Good primary sources include the Christ Church Parish Vestry Book and the Lancaster County records. The church was, with the county government, the complementary authoritarian entity in the colony. By law, a vestry (the first vestry was elected and it was self-perpetuating from within its ranks after that) under the leadership of two church wardens, dealt with the moral and certain temporal issues of the community. They collected the tithes, which maintained the church, paid the rector's salary and cared for impoverished widows and orphaned children. Church attendance at a minimum of one service a month was mandatory, and a fine was imposed for several successive absences.

[16]Lancaster County Court Order Book 8:192.

[17]Robert Carter Diary 1722-1728, Sunday, 21 July 1723. Transcribed from a partially corrected, typed transcript property of the University of Virginia Library, lent by Francis L. Berkeley, solely for reference and research use by the Historic Christ Church Foundation volunteers.

[18]Edwards, *Doctor Richard Edwards*, 21.

[19]Mary Ruth Stultz, *Ingram Family History, From England to America* (privately published, undated, copyright 1985) Mary Ball Washington Museum and Library, 111.

[20]Ibid.

[21]Lancaster County Court Order Book 6:342 records the order on 10 May 1721 that Catherine Dare deliver to Thomas Edwards, Clerk of the Court, "all records belonging to the Court." She waited three years to do so, turning them over on 8 April 1724, at which time a list was made of the bound volumes and their contents and notice taken of the parcel of bundles of loose papers. See also Lancaster County Court Order Book 8:277 and Lancaster County Deed Book 13:272.

[22]Lancaster County Will Book 16:80. Edwards had named Landon Carter, son of Robert "King" Carter, as Trustee of his estate. In his will, Edwards wrote, "I request my Esteemed and constant friend, Landon Carter, Esq. to be aiding and assisting to them [Edwards' children] and do hereby enjoin every of my children to set down by his ultimate decision." The warm relationship with several of the Carter sons is an interesting juxtaposition to his less-than-amicable early relationship with their father.

[23]Edwards, *Dr. Richard Edwards*.

[24]Lancaster County Court Order Book 9:114.

[25]Lancaster County Deed and Will Book 14:131.

[26]Lancaster County Marriage Register, 1715-1832.

[27]Lancaster County Court Order Book 9:134.

[28]Lancaster County Deed Book 14:165.

[29]Lancaster County Will book 16:80.

[30]Lancaster County Will Book 14:131.

JAMES WRIGHT MANUMITTED SLAVE

Perhaps the most anonymous segment of society in Christ Church parish was the African-American population. Circumstances of enslavement as well as barriers of language, education, and religion meant that these people appeared only rarely in either the public or private records of the time. James Wright was an exception, but even when all the clues of his relatively short life are pieced together, the reader leaves with more questions than answers.

Wright was born into the anonymity of slavery about 1721. His owner was Henry Fleet III of Lancaster County. Fleet lived in the upper echelon of local society. He owned a substantial amount of land and numerous slaves. His grandfather, Henry Fleete, had immigrated to Virginia in the first half of the 17th century and was one of the first two Burgesses to represent Lancaster after its formation in 1651.[1]

When Fleet died in 1735 he made some very specific distributions of his property through his will. He left explicit instructions about 23 slaves, including Wright. However, 14-year-old Wright was the only slave to whom he promised freedom. "My will is that my negro boy James serve the said Rebecca Banton till he attains the age of twenty-four years, and that she then obtain his freedom as the law requires."[2]

The fact that Rebecca Banton was to be Wright's new owner only deepens the mystery. Fleet obviously held Banton in high regard, as he left her his plantation and eight other slaves. If Banton were related to Fleet or involved with him in some other way, those answers have not been discovered. Further, the question of why Fleet chose to free a 14-year-old slave and not provide any such stipulations for the other 22 slaves mentioned in his will is another mystery.

Ten years later, in November 1745, Banton carried out Fleet's final wishes and freed Wright when he turned 24.

Manumitting a slave was not something to be taken lightly in colonial Virginia, for the law was very specific about such acts. In 1723 the Virginia Assembly stipulated "that no negro, mullatto, or indian slaves, shall be set free, upon any pretence, whatsoever, except for some meritorious services, to be adjudged and allowed by the governor and council, for the time being, and a licence thereupon first had and obtained."[3]

Fleet must have been well aware of this law when he penned his will, which is probably why he carefully worded his request to be "as the law requires." Banton would also have been aware of the law, especially as the time for Wright's freedom neared. Obviously she could not simply request that her slave be freed. Rather, she had to petition Virginia's colonial governor and prove that Wright had performed "some meritorious services."

The petition that Banton sent to Williamsburg was carefully worded and included a sound reason for Wright's[4] manumission, but whether it was all true or concocted to fit the letter of the law will never be known. Fleet, she wrote, "had a great Regard for the Said Slave on account of his Fedelity and good Service. . . ."[5]

The manumission of Wright leaves several questions. What fidelity and good service could Wright have possibly provided by the age of 14 that some of the older slaves had not provided? Was there, perhaps, an unwritten reason why Wright received preferential treatment? Nothing has yet surfaced to answer these questions, so any answers are merely speculation.

What kind of life did Wright lead during those 24 years? Was he a privileged house slave or did he have a trade that made him a craftsman? Did other slaves resent his status? By the 1740s there were more than 1,000 blacks over the age of 16 living in Lancaster County, but Wright's status and lifestyle were not the norm.[6] He certainly would have been different from the majority of blacks living in the community. For one, the manumission petition describes him as "A Negro Boy Slave Christend James"[7] which means that he was a practicing Christian and perhaps taking communion.[8]

Possible preferential treatment and Christianity aside, Wright's status as a slave gave him very few options in life and even fewer rights. Gatherings of slaves were prohibited, even for something as simple as a religious service, unless owners' permissions were first obtained. Those who violated the law were dealt with harshly. If guns or other weapons were found in the possession of slaves, lashes on a bare back were the result. Slaves who were chronic runaways could be physically maimed, and owners whose slaves died while being legally "corrected" were not accountable for manslaughter. Under Virginia law, if five or more slaves gathered together and discussed rebelling, or if they plotted a murder or committed a felony, they could be executed or dismembered without benefit of clergy.[9]

Even after obtaining his freedom in 1745, Wright existed as a second-class citizen. He now had to join the militia but was not allowed to carry a weapon during those military turnouts. Instead he was used as a drummer, trumpeter, "pioneer" or in some "other servile labour." The word "pioneer" was not used in the same way then as it is today. Pioneers were those people employed in the manual labor of cutting brush and clearing roadways so that large groups of military men, animals, and even vehicles could maneuver for drilling purposes, encampment, or marching. All militia units across the colony would have had occasional need for such labor, and it was not often the sweat of the militia officers, but rather that of the pioneers, which was expended.[10]

Although Wright could own land, he could never aspire to vote. He could also be convicted of participating in an unlawful meeting if he gathered with his friends still in bondage. Technically, he could even be arrested and punished for visiting the plantation where his wife was a slave without first gaining permission of her owner. In reality, however, the slavery laws of the colony were administered unevenly. There were benevolent masters who bent the law in one direction and harsh owners who bent the law the other

The manumission of James Wright, which Rebecca Banton requested in fulfillment of Henry Fleet's will, was recorded in the Lancaster County courthouse as the legal document seen here.

way. For all of society, the existence of a rigid class system that included bondage meant maintaining a delicate balance because everyone, black, white, or mulatto, was trapped by the legal structure of the colony.

In addition to being able to own land as a freedman, Wright gained a number of legal privileges and was now allowed to own one gun — something he did, for a gun is listed in his estate inventory. Little is known about the dozen years Wright spent as a freedman. There is no record that he ever owned land; more than likely he settled on Banton's plantation. In 1746 he appears by name as her tithable. In 1747 Banton officially discharged "her Negroe Man James from further service"[11] though Banton and Wright remained in close contact whether through obligation or friendship. One can only wonder if the 1742 Lancaster grand jury presentment against Banton for "feasting and harbouring negroes at her house" was a social gathering in which Wright, her slave at the time, was present.[12] We know from Wright's estate inventory that he probably was a musician of sorts as an old fiddle and strings were listed among his belongings. Could he have provided music at social gatherings?[13]

When she wrote her will in 1750, Banton took care to provide for her former slave. After devising a number of small gifts, she stipulated that "all the rest of my estate [go to] James Right who formerly Belonged to me further my will is that the estate be sold and William Bond have the charge of the money to let him have it as he wants It or Wm. Bond shall think Proper."[14] The amount Banton devised to Wright was probably not substantial. The 250-acre plantation she inherited from Fleet for her lifetime reverted to a Fleet heir at her death. Banton also inherited 50 percent of Fleet's personal estate, but again that was for her use during her lifetime. The remainder reverted to Samuel Hinton, Fleet's nephew by marriage, who had inherited the other half of the personal estate in Fleet's will.[15] Anything Wright inherited would have been income generated from the estate through Banton's investments, agricultural production, or items purchased with that income.

An inventory of Wright's estate, taken in 1757, provides some insight into those dozen years of freedom and indicates that he might have plied the area waters as a mariner. Included in the list are "the half of one old Schooner,[16] halfe of a marinors Compass,[17] 1 old canoe and a parcell of old cloths [could these have been sails?], and an old fish gigg."[18] The existence of the compass means that Wright was doing more than operating a ferry (which the canoe with sails could very well have been) or sailing the local rivers. He probably ventured at least into the more open waters of the Chesapeake Bay and maybe beyond.

At some point Wright married Sarah, a slave who was owned by Nicholas Currell.[19] The Currells lived on a plantation in the same vicinity as Banton's land, and Nicholas Currell was Henry Fleet III's nephew.[20] Thomas Perkins, an area mariner featured in an earlier biography in this book, had married into the Currell family so perhaps Wright found work within the family circle. It would be interesting to know who held the other half interest in the schooner and compass.

James and Sarah Wright had at least four children: James, Spencer, Betty, and Kendal. One can only wonder if Wright yearned for the freedom of his family once he had been freed or if the Currells would have been open to the idea of manumission for the entire family. Regardless of the answers, it was not an option. Upon his death in 1757, Wright had accumulated at least £23 and had an estate inventory valued at more than £12. At a time when slaves were valued at £20 - £40, he probably had enough  to buy his wife had the opportunity been presented. But Virginia law was very clear on the matter: manumission took place only under extraordinary circumstances and through a petition to the Virginia governor. The relaxation of this law did not occur until 1782 when the Virginia Assembly decided to allow private manumissions through deeds and wills.[21]

The provocative story of James Wright came to a close in 1757 when he died at the approximate age of 36. He left a will signed with his mark, meaning he was probably unable to write. The value of his estate was laudable for a man who had spent two-thirds of his life in bondage. To his wife he left "three pounds Credit in a Store," while he gave each of his four children, all owned by Nicholas Currell, £5 when they turned 18. His daughter also received his bed and furniture. The remaining devisees were white men who were relatives of Henry Fleet III, Wright's original owner. Richard Hinton received a black horse, while William Hinton was given a saddle and harness. The rest of his estate, which Banton had willed to him, went to Samuel Hinton, who was also his executor.[22] In addition to the watermen's tools and fiddle listed in Wright's inventory, there were two head of cattle, a pair of boots, stockings, two old chests, an old tub, an old pot, two old rugs (bed coverings), an old blanket, an old silk purse, a lock and key, nearly £2 of cash, a clasp knife (pocket knife), a jugg, and a gun. There are absolutely no agricultural items included beyond the two cattle, giving further credence to Wright making a living from the water. His family's food source would have come in the form of rations given by the Currells but could have been supplemented by any fishing and hunting that Wright did and through any garden that the family was allowed to keep at the Currell plantation. Wright's inventory was taken by Nicholas Currell, who owned Wright's family, Thomas Hunton, and Roger Kelley. All three men lived in the upper part of Fleet's Neck and Wright lived on Fleet's Island.

We know more about James Wright than we do about most other African-Americans of 18th-century Lancaster County. When he died he was a "free, negroe, Christian," who had lived his life first in the anonymity of slavery and then in the shadows of second-class citizenship as a free black man. He may be buried on Fleet's Island where Banton's plantation was located. The fate of his family remains uncertain. Without Wright's status as a free man to connect with, they finished out the remainder of their lives as slaves and died without their surnames ever being recorded. Nicholas Currell, who in 1757 owned Wright's wife, Sarah, as well as their four children, died in June 1801. By that time Virginia had gone from being a colony to being a state and manumission laws had been slightly relaxed. Currell's estate included at least 36 slaves. Among the list were some tantalizing names: two Spencers, two Sarahs, an Eliza (Betty?), a Kendall, and a James. James was among three slaves who were freed in the will.[23] Was this James the son of James Wright? If so, he achieved freedom 56 years after Rebecca Banton had fulfilled the dying wishes of her friend Henry Fleet III by petitioning the Virginia governor for James Wright's freedom. The other slaves with first names that indicate possible connections to the Wright story were all willed to Currell's relatives.

ENDNOTES

[1] FHCCRF - Parish Profile Archives. It is the careful gathering and piecing together of documents and clues from researchers associated with the Parish Profile project that have allowed Wright's story to come to light.

[2] Henry Fleet will, 26 November 1735, Lancaster County Will Book 12:358.

[3] William Waller Hening, *The Statutes at Large; Being a collection of all the Laws of Virginia* (New York: Printed for the Editor, By R&W&G Bartow, 1823, facsimile reprint published in 1969 for the Jamestown Foundation of the Commonwealth of Virginia by the University Press of Virginia, Charlottesville, Va.), 9 Geo. I. c.iv, May 1723, 4:132.

[4] Wright's name is spelled variously Right and Wright in Lancaster records.

[5] Lancaster County Deed and Will Book 14:100, 4 November 1745.

[6] Robert Anthony Wheeler, "Lancaster County, Virginia, 1650-1750: the Evolution of a Southern Tidewater Community" (Ph.D. thesis, Brown University, 1972), 142.

[7] Lancaster County Deed and Will Book 14:100, 4 November 1745.

[8] John Bell, the Christ Church rector from 1711-1743, noted in his 1724 report to the Bishop of London that many of the slaves in the parish were infidels who did not speak English. Despite that, he noted that "The Church is open to them; the word preached, and the Sacraments administered with circumspection."

[9] Hening, May 1723, 126-134. A person who claimed the "benefit of clergy" could use the law to exempt himself from capital punishment if he was a member of the clergy, a clerk, or was simply literate. A slave, even if he were literate, could not escape justice in this manner for most capital crimes. Henry Campbell Black, *Black's Law Dictionary*, Sixth Edition (St. Paul, Minn.: 1990), 158.

[10] Hening, May 1738, 17.

[11] Lancaster County Court Order Book 9:150.

[12] The court dismissed the presentment in December 1742. Lancaster County Court Order Book 8:364, 369.

[13] Lancaster Deed and Will Book 16:6.

[14] Lancaster County Will Book 15:303. Bond was also a devisee of Banton's, having received "one Bed and Bedstead and all the Furniture thereto Belonging which stands in the Little House," as well as a gold ring and a punch bowl.

[15] Lancaster County Will Book 12:358.

[16]Presumably this means he had half interest in the ownership of the schooner, described as "old," a term which might explain the relatively low value of that portion of ownership which was £5.

[17]The same assumption must be made for the mariner's compass which was valued at five shillings.

[18]The discovery of this inventory, which does not appear in any of the indexes but is recorded in Lancaster County Deed and Will Book 16:6, was made by a Parish Profile researcher. The document was proved in court on 18 November 1757 and recorded on 21 April 1758.

[19]It is possible that when Wright married Sarah she was owned by Thomas Lawson and simply lived within the Currell household. Lawson died in August 1747. His inventory included 14 slaves, among whom were Sarah, Kendal, and James. Five of the 14 slaves were to be sold to pay Lawson's debts. Did Nicholas Currell purchase James Wright's family at that time? Wright's will, written in 1753, states that his wife and children were "now in the Possession of Mr. Nicholas Currell." Does this mean that Currell owned them or that Currell was hiring them and that they were living in Currell's household because he had a rental agreement with Lawson? Ultimately it doesn't matter because Lawson's widow, Margaret Steptoe Lawson, married Nicholas Currell in July 1750. Thomas Lawson will, Lancaster County Deed and Will Book 14:47; James Right will, Lancaster County Will Book 15:621; FHCCRF - James Wright file.

[20]Henry Fleet III's sister, Elizabeth, married Abraham Currell and their son was Nicholas, owner of Wright's wife.

[21]Allan Kulikoff, *Tobacco and Slaves: The Development of Southern Cultures in the Chesapeake, 1680-1800* (Chapel Hill, N.C.: Published for the Institute of Early American History and Culture, Williamsburg, Va., by the University of North Carolina Press, 1986), 432.

[22]Lancaster County Will Book 15:621.

[23]Lancaster County Will Book 28:49.

JOHN BUCKLES, OVERSEER
JAMES ROB, CARPENTER

When James Rob advertised for his runaway servant, Stephen Chelson, in 1746 in the Virginia Gazette, he was an established landowner and businessman in Lancaster County protecting his business interest against loss. His apprentice, 19-year-old Chelson, was in the third year of his apprenticeship as a carpenter and furniture maker and his disappearance would certainly hurt the production of Rob's shop.[1] What the short advertisement does not reveal is that Rob was not always in such a position of authority. An intense look into the scattered records left concerning Rob and his family help create the image of a self-made man who used the relative mobility of early 18th-century Chesapeake society together with a wise marriage choice to move up in the social order.

The first public mention of Rob occurred in Robert Carter's inventory taken after his death in August 1732. On page 13 of that extensive inventory, Rob appears as one of 17 white servants living at Carter's home plantation. Rob is described as a carpenter on a list with a number of other craftsmen, including another carpenter, a glassier, two tailors, a gardener, a blacksmith, two bricklayers, and a sailor. Part of this assemblage may have been created by Carter as a workforce for the new church he was building for Christ Church Parish.[2]

On the 17th page of the inventory is the name of another man whose destiny became entwined with that of Rob – John Buckles. Buckles was an overseer at the Corotoman Quarter, across the creek from the main plantation, where he and his family probably resided in a simple, story-and-a-half earthfast dwelling that consisted of two rooms on each floor. His employment was already established by 1723, for on April 20 of that year Carter noted that he "gve Buckles some thred for his people."[3] Periodic mention of Buckles occurs thereafter in the diary including a 1723 instance in which Buckles visited Carter about a discipline problem with one "Josh Harrison." Carter's reaction to his overseer's report was to take the offender before a magistrate and have him whipped.[4]

By 1733, Buckles was in charge of 19 black slaves who would have lived in duplex-type, multiple family dwellings within close proximity to each other and to the overseer's house. Included in the quarter was Charles, a foreman, and his wife, Norah. The foreman was the slave who was second-in-command to the white overseer on a plantation. In addition to the slaves, the quarter contained 35 pigs, 30 sheep, an old mare named Spott, and 55 cattle. Inside the cabins were some standard issue items belonging to the estate: a large "pott" and hooks, an old "pott," a pestle, two wedges, and a grindstone. Because Buckles was free, his personal cooking utensils probably are not those listed in the estate inventory. Those listed were probably found either in the foreman's household or scattered among the other cabins.[5]

By 1733, Buckles may not have lived at the Corotoman Quarter at all, but left the daily direction of the hands to his foreman, Charles. As late as 1727, however, it appears that Buckles and his family had still been living on the quarter. In December 1727, Carter visited the complex and noted: "At Buckles he & his wife at home, a great many people there, 7 hgs in the pen, 35 sheep."[6]

By 1721 Buckles owned 135 acres but whether his family was living there or in an overseer's house in 1733 is not known.[7] Buckles' plantation, which he actively farmed, was on Corotoman Neck in Christ Church Parish Precinct F. This was across the river from Corotoman Quarter. Either way the Buckles family would have been in daily contact with the other servants, black and white, living in the parish.

Certainly Buckles' four daughters were noticed by a young servant named James Rob. Rob was probably an indentured servant brought from England in one of Carter's periodic recruitments of trained craftsmen. He would have been at least 21 years of age to have completed an appren-

Perhaps James Rob dressed in a fashion similar to the 18th-century joiner, or carpenter, depicted in this woodcut.

ticeship in England and probably closer to 30 in 1733. Rob's indenture had expired by December 1733 because indentured servants were not allowed to marry. On January 9, 1734, Rob married Frances, the eldest daughter of John Buckles. John Buckles and Thomas Machen were security and witness for the Lancaster County marriage bond of these two parishioners of Christ Church Parish.[8]

More than likely the match pleased the widower Buckles,[9] as he must have worried about the dispersal of his property, both personal and real, with four daughters. When he died a few months later in 1734,[10] his three youngest daughters, Ann, Lucey, and Margaret, were all under the age of 21. Buckles, who was illiterate, directed in his will that tobacco be used to contract with a tutor named Michael Ryan, who would educate his daughters.

Buckles' eldest daughter inherited the bulk of the estate, and her new husband served as one of the estate's two executors, the other being Buckles' friend, William Edmonds. The plantation went to Frances with the stipulation that the plantation house remain a home to her three siblings until they were married. A slave named Jo was left to work the plantation until all of the daughters married or reached their majority, at which time one daughter was to keep Jo and reimburse her siblings for his value. All of the cattle from the farm also went to the Robs, but the hogs were to be equally divided among the four daughters. While Buckles had accumulated a number of nice belongings, we will never know the exact extent of his holdings because he requested that his estate not be appraised, which means no inventory was taken. He doled out several pieces of furniture and everyday household goods including some bedsteads, chests, an oval table, pewter, and pots to his three younger daughters. In addition they inherited silver studs, a gold ring, and some silver buckles. A measure of Buckles' status in the community can be drawn from the witness to his will: Henry Carter, John Merideth, and Robert Carter (not Robert "King" Carter).[11]

If the Robs were not already living on Buckles' Corotoman Neck plantation before March 1734, they were after that time. The 1748 rent roll lists Rob as the owner of the same 134-acre tract which belonged to Buckles in 1721.[12]

Within a few years, Rob had gone from the role of servant to that of prospering tradesman and landholder. In 1746 there were six tithables at his house, a number which certainly included several slaves and indentured servants. How many of his sisters-in-law continued to reside there is unknown. At least one, Ann Buckles, never married, and upon her death in 1776 she gave much of her modest estate to her sister Frances Rob and some nieces and nephews.[13]

The two Buckles sisters outlived James Rob by many years. However, the 2½-page, double column inventory taken at his death in 1747 tells a tale of prosperity achieved in the relatively short period of 13 years. The list included three slaves, Joe (who had been inherited from John Buckles), Martha, and Ben. Martha had been part of the household for at least a decade because the Lancaster County Court had decided in July 1737 that Martha was, at that time, 13 years old. Because slave owners were required to pay tithes, or taxes, on blacks age 16 and older, the court's determination was important for tax purposes and also helps later researchers learn a few small details about Martha.[14]

Perhaps Rob was not a particularly benevolent taskmaster because Chelson (Chilton) was not the only servant to run away. In 1736 Timothy Collins, "a Servant man belonging to James Rob," confessed to having run away for five days. After Rob testified that he had spent 200 pounds of tobacco in recovering Collins, the court ordered the servant to serve an additional three months and 10 days after his indenture had expired.[15]

From the time that he handled his father-in-law's estate, which included some debt settlement, Rob was a contributing member of Lancaster society. He served on a grand jury four times in the 1730s. In 1735 he found himself on a jury listening to the case of a bricklayer named William Oliver who felt he had been cheated out of his money by Thomas Bridgeford. Perhaps remembering his own days as a simple tradesman, Rob and the rest of the jury decided in favor of Oliver but not for the entire amount.[16] As any neighbor of good standing would do, Rob also helped appraise an estate and witnessed a will within the community.

Not content with the status quo, Rob sought ways to increase his wealth. In the late 1730s he petitioned the court to "turn" or reroute the road leading through his plantation to-

James Rob placed this advertisement in the "Virginia Gazette" in 1746 after his apprentice, Stephen Chelson, ran away.

ward Mr. Edward's mill. A report generated by the court decided that the proposed road would not inconvenience any of Rob's neighbors and gave him permission to clear a good road as he proposed and then to close down the old road.[17]

When Rob died in 1747, he left a substantial estate valued at approximately £175. The fact that he had close to 20 books, including a divinity book, as well as paper and ink powder, hints that he was literate. His wife, on the other hand, signed the estate appraisal with just a mark, indicating that she was probably not literate. Perhaps Buckles' provision for the education of his daughters did not extend to Frances, who was already married, or perhaps the education was for reading only but not for writing.

In addition to the three slaves in Rob's inventory, there were three horses and two carts. There was also a riding saddle for his wife and himself. Not surprisingly, there was a large group of "new & old carpenters and Joynes Tools in a Chest with lock & Key," as well as "1 New Carpenters Rule" and an old rule. There were also handsaw files and gimblets. More surprising is the large number of dry goods and sewing supplies listed in the inventory. There were more than 100 yards of textiles listed, which is probably more than was needed to keep his household clothed but not enough to be operating as a merchant. Was one of his slaves a tailor or seamstress whom he was using to produce clothing? Was he accepting dry goods as a type of barter? The answer to this will probably never be known.[18]

What can be read from the records is the success Rob made of his life. If, indeed, he came from England as an indentured servant, it was a wise choice. His marriage brought land and a family. His children included at least Sarah, who married Job Carter, the son of Joseph Carter; Margaret, who never married; probably Lucy, who married Jesse Robinson of Northumberland County; probably Thomas Rob; and maybe Agatha Rob.[19] By the time of his death in 1747, Rob may have moved further up the social ladder and accumulated more wealth and land than would have been possible had he remained in the land of his birth.

ENDNOTES

[1]*Virginia Gazette*, Thursday, 26 June 1746. The name Chelson is almost certainly Chelton or Chilton, a family which had been in Lancaster since the 17th century.

[2]Robert Carter inventory, 13.

[3]Robert Carter Diary 1722-1728, 20 April 1723. Transcribed from a partially corrected, typed transcript property of the University of Virginia Library, lent by Francis L. Berkeley, solely for reference and research use by the Historic Christ Church Foundation volunteers.

[4]Ibid., July 1, 1723.

[5]Robert Carter inventory.

[6]Robert Carter Diary 1722-1728, December 1727. Transcribed from a partially corrected, typed transcript property of the University of Virginia Library, lent by Francis L. Berkeley, solely for reference and research use by the Historic Christ Church Foundation volunteers.

[7]Christ Church Parish, Lancaster County, Virginia, Rent Rolls 1721, copies at FHCCRF, used with permission of The Huntington Library, San Marino, California. Buckles purchased one of his parcels of land from John Tayloe in 1716. Lancaster County Deed and Will Book 11:71.

[8]The length of an indenture was anywhere from four to seven years, and Rob was near the end of his indenture in 1733. Therefore, the youngest he could have been was 25, assuming a four-year indenture, but he could have been 28 assuming a seven-year indenture. He could also have worked for a few years in England before coming to Virginia which, conceivably, could put him well into his 30s. Lancaster County Marriage List, 9 January 1733, list contained in FHCCRF.

[9]Buckles' wife, whose name is unknown, apparently died sometime between 1727, when Robert Carter mentions seeing her, and 1734, when Buckles died without mention of a wife.

[10]Because the new year was calculated from March 25, Buckles' death could have been in early March 1734 or March 1735. Sometimes the clerk recorded the date as 1734/35 but in this instance the date was only recorded as 1735. Until 1752, the legal new year in the colonies was March 25.

[11]Lancaster County Will Book 12:332-333.

[12]Lancaster County Will Book 12:332; 1748 rent roll (Note: the 1750 rent roll has Rob with 130 acres).

[13]Lancaster County Will Book 20:88, 96.

[14]James Rob inventory, Nov. 13, 1747, Lancaster County Deed and Will Book 14:160-162; Lancaster County Court Order Book, 1729-1743, July 8, 1737, 177.

[15]Lancaster County Court Order Book 8, July 14, 1736, 148.

[16]Lancaster County Court Order Book 8, 124, 14 April 1735.

[17]Ibid., 91, 94.

[18]Rob inventory.

[19]Lancaster County Marriage Register, 36, Sarah Rob to Job Carter, January 11, 1768; Margaret Rob's will, Lancaster County Will Book 20:115, June 18, 1777; Lancaster County Marriage Register, 32, Lucy Robb to Jesse Robinson, May 21, 1764; Thomas Robb's will, Lancaster County Will Book 20:219, January 17, 1782.

THE MAUGHON FAMILY

Some landowning families in Christ Church such as Conway, Edwards, and Fleet experienced success and comfort for several generations. For others, who owned very small holdings, life was difficult, and poverty never far from the door. The Maughon family is a well-documented example of a close-knit but poor family that held together in the parish for several generations.

The surname appears with rich variety in the Lancaster County records: Maughon, Moughone, Mahan, Mahone, Mahoon, Mahoane, Mohon, suggesting two possible pronunciations, the single-syllable Maughon, like Vaughan, and the two-syllable Mahone. In either case, the name would appear to be of Irish origin.[1] It is hard to say when the first member of the family appeared in Lancaster County.

Patrick Maughon, a resident of Christ Church Parish from at least 1713, appears on the 1720 tithable list with two tithes, probably himself and an indentured servant, John Ollard, a tailor.[2] In this respect, he was a fairly typical landholder. More than half of the 146 heads of household in the parish that year had only one or two tithables, and of those 75, Patrick Maughon was one of the 34 who owned land.

When the parish vestry processioned the land in 1719, checking the boundaries in the presence of owners, Maughon's holding of 50 acres appeared in Precinct A adjacent to Thomas Griggs's 50-acre holding and to one tract of the 600-acre holding of William Dymer, a gentleman and member of the vestry.[3] His land was part of the Bonnison tract of 1,300 acres that extended from the western part of Precinct A across Poplar Neck.[4] The exceptionally wealthy Carter family had tracts nearby such as Hills Quarter. Patrick Mahoane acquired this 50-acre tract in deeds of lease and release signed on October 9 and 10, 1713, with Richard Harrell (Harwell, Harrowell), whose father had acquired the land in 1682 from

Thomas Bonnison. The adjacent 50 acres was purchased at that time by Thomas Griggs, with the understanding that Griggs was to have half of the fruit in the old orchard on Maughon's land.[5]

Patrick Maughon probably acquired this land at the time he and Frances Brush married. Frances was a daughter of William Brush, a small landholder in Precinct C, and sister of William and Abel Brush. As early as 1678, a William Brush, possibly Frances's grandfather, appeared on the Christ Church Parish tithable list with one tithable. The appraisal of the estate of a William Brush was recorded on August 9, 1709 at a value of £45:06:11. From 1691 to 1720 the name William Brush appears regularly with one or two tithables. In January 1710, William Brush acquired 50 acres in Precinct C in a proprietor's deed. In 1731, after the death of her brother, Abel, Frances acquired this 50-acre tract and later gave it to her son, William.[6]

Absolom Maughon, the first child, was born about 1714. Catherine and one unnamed child in public records followed him, then William in 1719 and baby Patrick in 1721. Patrick Maughon died in the fall of 1721, probably suddenly, for he left no will. In his estate administration records and in the provisions for his minor children, we are able to see something of the very modest daily lives of this family and the many like them in the parish who managed a simple self-sufficiency. Frances Mohon (Maughon) was administratrix of her husband's estate and she posted £100 bond, with the help of James Carter and Robert Gibson, to provide a full inventory.[7] Neighbors and friends William Dymer, William Martin, and John Angel appraised the personal estate.

Patrick Maughon had died in possession of one indentured servant, John Olord (Allard), whose remaining term of service as a tailor was valued at £6:10:00. His livestock consisted of three cows with calves, one cow with a yearling, two cows without young, one young steer, and three yearlings. Their total value of nearly £15 made them by far his most valuable possessions. He must have engaged the services of a neighbor's bull each year. The livestock suggests that much of his land was given to grazing for cattle and possibly for dairy production, rather than the cultivation of tobacco. He also owned a young mare, so he had transportation, but no saddle.

The meager furnishings of the house suggest that it was a two-room, earthfast structure that was the most typical kind of housing in colonial Virginia.[8] For furniture, the family possessed one old bedstead, an old couch, a "feather bed & furneture," and a "flock bed & furneture," which was ticking filled with shorn wool. The furniture consisted of the fabric items, such as curtains and a valance, associated with a bed. On these, the two parents, five children and one servant had to sleep. They had one table and "forms" (benches), one large chest, and one old trunk. The cooking pots were weighed, rather than enumerated, amounting to 116 pounds. Similarly, their dishes, mostly of pewter, were weighed: 12 pounds of better quality at 10 pence a pound and 14 pounds of old pewter at six pence a pound, in addition to a parcel of earthenware. There were two spits for roasting meat and fowl. A spinning wheel indicated that Frances kept busy at that feminine task, among many others. The tools consisted of three iron wedges, one ax, and one grindstone. Patrick Maughon had some weapons, an old "sord" and a "pistoll," and some cider casks (to make use of his half share of the fruit in the old orchard on his property), and tubs and pails, likely for dairying activities.[9]

The young widow, with five minor children to support, was undoubtedly eager to remarry. By at least 1727 Frances Brush Maughon had married John Brooks, for the processioners' returns of that year show John Brooks's land adjacent to Dymer and Griggs. They became the parents of one daughter. Little is known about Brooks. In 1726 he witnessed the will of Robert

Angell, member of a family that was closely tied with the Maughons. In 1729 the county court dismissed a suit he brought against Robert Thompson.[10]

In 1731, after the death of her brother, Abel Brush, Frances and her husband, John Brooks, brought suit against her sister-in-law, Mary Brush, administratrix of Abel's estate, claiming that Frances, as heir of her father, William Brush, was to receive two-thirds of the real estate and one-half of the personal property. The value of the personal property was exceedingly modest, £17:17:01, fewer possessions than Patrick Maughon had willed a decade earlier, but to a person of limited possessions and five young children, even half of that was welcome.[11]

In 1732, guardians' accounts were recorded for the three sons of Frances and Patrick Maughon. As orphans (children of a deceased father even though the mother might be living), the law required that a guardian look after their property interests and sometimes to see that they received appropriate education and job training. John Angell was the guardian for Absolom Maughon. Angell was probably a weaver, for that is the trade Absolom later practiced and for which an apprentice was bound to him. Absolom's guardian inventory, recorded in 1732, consisted of one cow and calf, one flock bed, and one gun, with a total value of £4:9:0. By 1735, Absolom was a landowner in the parish and so was at least 21 years old, meaning that he was born about 1714.[12]

John Wale was the guardian of the two younger Maughon boys, William and Patrick. William, 13, and Patrick, 11, in 1732 were only two years old and a few months respectively when their father died. Their stepfather, John Brooks, was the only father they really knew. William was apprenticed to Wale to learn the trade of a carpenter, as well as to read and write. Patrick, who had turned 11 on June 9, 1732, was apprenticed to Wale to learn the trade of weaver, just like Absolom.[13] The inventory of the two younger brothers shows a total value of £8:18:0, indicating that the three boys had equal shares from their father's estate. Their combined inventory included a cow and yearling, a steer and a heifer, one large chest, a grind stone, three cider casks, two old hoes, three sides of tanned leather, a large iron pot, three iron wedges, a pestle, an ax, 1¼ pounds pewter, and 10 pence, which John Angell was holding for them.[14] Their father's total personal estate had been valued at £35:26:02. When his widow's obligatory third, £11:22, was deducted, the balance of £22:24 allowed each of the five children to receive £4:9:0.

Absolom Maughon, who had reached his majority in 1735, married Susannah, daughter of John Angell, the man to whom Absolom had been apprenticed. Before 1744, William married Rebecca Angell, another daughter of John. The ties between the Maughon and Angell families were long and strong, encompassing friendship, guardianship, apprenticeship, and intermarriage. When John Angell died in early March 1745, his executor and his elder son, Uriah Angell, presented an estate inventory valued at £46:17:10 for the personal property and £148:0:0 for the five slaves. The personal possessions were more numerous and of better quality than those in the inventories of Patrick Maughon and his brother-in-law, Abel Brush. They included more livestock — sheep and hogs as well as cattle — beds complete with curtains and valences, a looking glass, trundle beds for the children, chairs rather than benches for sitting at the table, craftsmen's tools, a loom, better farming equipment, a "Common Prayer Book," a sermon book, and several other books. As these possessions were divided among the Angell children, the two Maughon sons came into some of them by right of their marriage into the family.[15] In 1750, the court named Absolom Maughon the guardian for John Angell's minor son, Benoni, at the request of the boy.[16]

The two daughters of Frances and Patrick Maughon also married, though apparently not into families as stable or as well established in the parish as the Angells. Katherine married Thomas Lizenby (Lysenby) and moved to the Wicomico Parish section of Lancaster County. He died in 1745, leaving his widow with three young children.[17] The other daughter married Thomas O'Harrow (Harrow, O'Hara?). When he died in 1764, the appraisers of his estate were three men in the Windmill

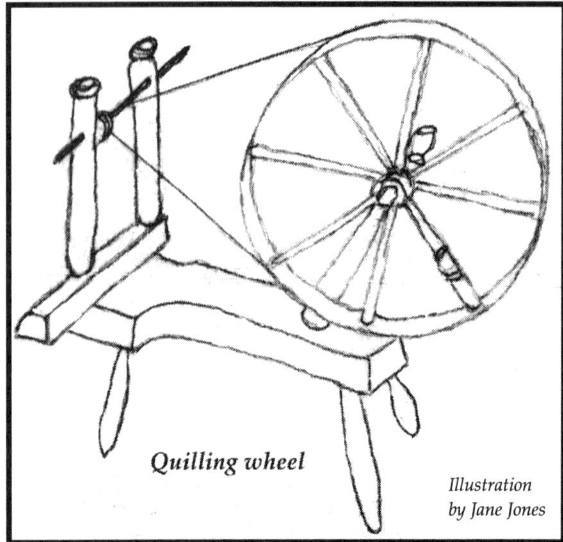

Quilling wheel

Illustration by Jane Jones

Point area, indicating that the family lived nearby. The presence of a small boat, rigging, and clamp tongs in his inventory suggests that he made his living as a waterman. His small estate was divided between the widow and his 10 children. If that widow was the daughter of Patrick and Frances Maughon, it can only be assumed that she inherited a difficult life and had dropped in status from even the modest circumstances of her birth family.

Absolom Maughon came into the 50-acre tract that had been his parents' home. In 1741, Frances, by then widow of John Brooks, made a deed of gift to her second son, William Mahone (Maughon), giving him the 50-acre tract that she had inherited from her father, William Brush, through the estate of her brother, Abel.[18] When she died in 1744, Absolom was administrator of her meager estate, valued at £16:10:01. Each of the children received an equal share, and "the gerle" as her daughter by Brooks was listed, received use of what she needed.

Absolom was the most successful of the five Maughon siblings left fatherless so early. He and his wife, Susannah, were the parents of six children: sons James, John, George, and Mathias, and daughters Elizabeth and Susanna. They lived on the 50 acres where he was raised, but may have improved or replaced the little house his parents had. Absolom was sufficiently respected to be chosen a processioner for his precinct in 1743. He farmed, but he also practiced the trade his guardian and father-in-law, John Angell, had taught him. His weaving and textile equipment included two looms, seven slays, four shuttles, and three sets of weaving harness, a warping box, a quilting frame, a quill wheel (for winding spools of thread), a quilting frame, and three pairs of cotton and wool cards. He had an apprentice and was probably training at least one of his sons in weaving at the time he died in 1759. The amount of equipment he had on hand could have kept three or four persons working full time in aspects of textile production. His livestock included 17 sheep, essential to produce the wool he processed and wove. His inventory included substantial amounts of cotton, both picked and unpicked, but it is impossible to know if he grew that or purchased it. His two slaves, a man Will, and a girl, Winney, could handle farming, chores, and housework assistance, affording this Maughon family a better lifestyle than that of the previous generation.[19]

William Maughon, planter, made a deed of gift to his wife, Rebecca Angell Maughon, in 1762 for all the property in their house. The following year, the couple sold the 50 acres on which they lived and which his mother had so carefully fought to preserve to her family as a heritage from her father. William and Rebecca do not appear in the county records after 1763, so they may have struck out to find their fortune in western Virginia counties then attracting settlers with cheaper lands.

When Absolom died in 1759, his eldest son, James, inherited the 50-acre tract that Patrick had bought in 1713. When James died in 1774, he left the land to his brothers, John and George.[20] John, who lived in Gloucester County, and George, who lived elsewhere in Lancaster County, sold the land to George Brent in 1784. So it was that after nearly three-quarters of a century and four generations, there were no more Maughons among the small planters and marginal landholders of Christ Church Parish.

ENDNOTES

[1]Edward McLysaght, *The Surnames of Ireland* (Dublin: Irish Academic Press, 1985), passim. A Patrick Mahoon was a headright of John Pate and John Beverley in 1669, but he cannot be linked with the man of that name living in the parish from at least 1713. Nell Marion Nugent, *Cavaliers and Pioneers, Abstracts of Virginia Land Patents and Grants,* Volume II (Richmond: Virginia State Library, 1977), 57.

[2]Christ Church Parish, Lancaster County, Virginia, Rent Rolls 1720-1750, copies at FHCCRF, used with permission of The Huntington Library, San Marino, California; Christ Church Parish Tithable List of 1746, copy at the Virginia State Library and Archives, property of the Lancaster Court; Christ Church Parish Processioners returns, 1711-1783; Patrick Maughon will, dated 4 December 1721, probated 10 January 1721/22 lists "1 servant named John Olord." Lancaster County Will Book 10:340.

[3]"Processioners Returns 1711-1783, Christ Church Parish, Lancaster County," unpublished typescript. FHCCRF.

[4]Patent to Abya Bonnyson, Patent Book 4:297, 1661.

[5]Deeds of Lease and Release, 9 and 10 October 1713, recorded 14 October 1713. Lancaster County Deed Book 9:500.

[6]Grant to William Brush of 50 acres, 14 January 1709. Gray, Gertrude E., compiler, *Virginia Northern Neck Grants 1694-1742* (Baltimore: Genealogical Publishing Co., Inc., 1988), 42. William Brush was married to the widow of Richard Curtis, a property owner in Northumberland County, but we do not know if she was the mother of Frances Brush.

[7]Bond of £100 sterling for Frances Mohon, Admtrx. Of Patrick Mohon, dec'd. Lancaster County Will Book 10:340.

[8]Camille Wells, "The Eighteenth-Century Landscape of Virginia's Northern Neck," *Northern Neck of Virginia Historical Magazine* 37(December 1987), 4419-4421.

[9]Appraisal of Patrick Mohon Estate, 4 December 1721, recorded 10 January 1721/22, Lancaster County Will Book 10:344.

[10]"Processioners returns 1711-1783, Christ Church Parish; Robert Angell will, Lancaster County Will Book 10:512.

[11]Petition for Estate Division of Abel Brush, 14 April 1731, Lancaster County Order Book 8:32. Appraisal of Abel Brush, dec'd. Recorded 14 April 1731, Lancaster County Will Book 12:195.

[12]In 1745, John Reeves, orphan, was bound to Absolom Mahon until the age of 21 to learn the trade of a weaver. Lancaster County Court Order Book 9:66a. See the Priscilla Palmer Reeves biography earlier in this book.

[13]Apprenticeship contract of William Mohon to John Wale, carpenter, 1732; Apprenticeship contract of Patrick Mohon to John Wale, weaver, Lancaster County Court Order Book 8:63; Guardian inventory, 12 July 1732, Lancaster County Will Book 12:222.

[14]Guardians inventories and accounts for Absolum Mohon, and William and Patrick Mohon. Recorded 12 July 1732. Lancaster County Will Book 12:222.

[15]John Angell inventory, 10 May 1745, Lancaster County Deed and Will Book 14:73.

[16]Guardianship Order, Absolom Maughon for Benoni Angell, 8 June 1750, Lancaster County Court Order Book 9:217.

[17]Thomas Lizenby estate appraisal returned by Catherine Lizenby, 1745. Lancaster County Will Book 14:69. In the 1745 tithables list, Widow Lizenby appears with two tithables.

[18]Deed of gift, Frances Brooks to William Mahon, 1741, Lancaster County Deed and Will Book 13:229.

[19]Absolom Moughone inventory and appraisal, 21 September 1759, Lancaster County Will Book 16:73.

[20]Will of James Maughon. 1774, Lancaster County Will Book 20:78.

Rebecca Banton
Mysterious Woman of Wealth

The women of Christ Church Parish are far more elusive than the men of the parish, and far more difficult to document. Their legal status, following English custom and precedent, was largely subsumed under that of their male protectors, their fathers, husbands, or guardians. They had no public role, so they do not appear on lists of vestries, militia, voters, county court officers, processioners, road surveyors, or any similar records that help us to trace the lives of their fathers, husbands, and brothers. They appear infrequently in deeds, rent rolls, and tithable lists unless they are single heads of a household. Although some left a will, many did not, as provision for their support and for disposal of their husbands' estates had been made in their husbands' wills. Some women left behind a criminal record, and some were involved in suits, but they are a minority of the parish women.

Rebecca Banton is an interesting study, as there are both more records pertaining to her life and activities than for many women of the parish and because those records raise some interesting questions about social status, success, and security for women in early 18th-century Virginia.[1]

Her first appearance in the public record occurs with the administration of the estate of her father, Thomas Banton, who died in July 1698.[2] Her father may have been the Thomas Baynton who was an indentured servant to John Carter, father of Robert "King" Carter, and who had 10 months to serve when Carter's estate inventory was made in July 1670.[3] If so, he was not a person of high status in the community, for he was ordered to appear in court on several occasions to answer charges for which gentlemen were rarely summonsed. In 1671 the charge was getting a servant woman, Anne Ford, pregnant.[4] Twice in 1681 John Carter II brought charges of trespassing against Banton, and in 1687 he was charged with killing a marked hog.[5]

Rebecca was one of the three known children of Thomas Banton and his wife, Susanna Marshall, whom he had married by 1677.[6] Although no deeds have been found, Banton apparently acquired property, for processioning records mention "Bainton's old field" and "Banton's Swamp." Rebecca's sister, Elizabeth, married a respectable planter, Thomas Griggs, and had three daughters. Her mother must have died before her father. Edward, Rebecca's brother, died in November 1698, just five months after their father. He left his estate to Rebecca and to his goddaughter, Mary Haines, daughter of his administrator, James Haines.[7] Edward's share of their father's livestock and personal property would have come to Rebecca, making her a ward with a modest estate.

Apparently Rebecca was the youngest child, probably born in 1686, so she was not of age when her father died. Haines became her guardian. On September 9, 1702, probably right after her 16th birthday, Rebecca petitioned the court for possession of her estate which was in the hands of her guardian, James Haines. The next month, the court granted her the judgment of 1,940 pounds of tobacco from Haines.[8]

Rebecca Banton's whereabouts and activities for the next three decades are a total mystery. There is no indication at all whether she remained in the home of her guardian, moved out to live with her married sister, or established some other living arrangement. There is no indication that she ever married. The fact that she became a principal heir of a well-to-do bachelor from one of the county's most prominent families has yet to be explained.

When the bachelor Henry Fleet III died in 1735, Banton came into the use of a considerable estate for the remainder of her life, making her one of the most comfortably situated women in Christ Church Parish. Who was Henry Fleet III that he was in a position to elevate Banton from her modest past, and what was the nature of his bequest to her? Henry Fleet III, who bore the name of his father and grandfather, had a distinguished heritage from a gentry family of London and Kent. His great-grandfather was an original subscriber to the London Virginia Company, and his wife a cousin of Sir Francis Wyatt, Governor of Virginia from 1621 to 1624. His grandfather, then a young boy, came to Virginia in the governor's convoy. On a trading voyage up the Potomac in 1622, the boy was taken prisoner by Anacostan Indians, who held him for five years, during which time he learned their language. Henry Fleete I became an early fur trader and ship captain, acquired extensive lands in Lord Baltimore's new colony of Maryland, and played an important role in the capture of Chief Opechancanough after the 1644 uprising. He returned from England in 1648 with a wife and settled with her in what soon became Lancaster County. There he acquired more than 13,000 acres. He became the county's first Burgess, was lieutenant colonel of the militia, served as a justice of the county court, and was commissioner to settle differences with the Indians on the Northern Neck in 1653 and 1656. He died by 1661, leaving only his widow, Sarah, and one child, Henry Fleet II.[9]

Like his father before him, Henry Fleet II was a distinguished figure in Lancaster County. When he first married Elizabeth Wildey, by 1682, they lived in Northumberland County, but in 1691, they returned to his father's plantation on Fleet's Neck (not Fleet's Bay Neck) where he lived the remainder of his life. He served the county as justice, high sheriff, and was a major in the militia. Henry II and Elizabeth had seven known children, Henry Fleet, Jr. (III), and William, named for his maternal grandfather, and five daughters. In anticipation of the sons' marriages, Henry II gave each of them land in 1718. Henry III received 500 acres, the upper two quarters on Fleet's Island, while William received 300 acres, the lower quarter on the island, but never lived there, as he and his wife lived in King and Queen County. Henry III, however, settled on the upper quarter. His lower quarter he rented to Thomas Edwards, a weaver.[10]

Like the father and grandfather for whom he was named, Henry Fleet III took up public service as justice, sheriff, militia major, coroner, and surveyor of roads. He looked after his estate, socialized with his friends, including Robert "King" Carter, and kept a household on Fleet's Island that exemplified the new patterns of fashionable consumption that distinguished the wealthiest Virginia planters from their plainer neighbors. His card table, more than two dozen chairs, his large supply of brandy, his kitchen equipment, and tableware all indicated his position as a social leader in the upper level of Lancaster County planters. When he appeared at court as sheriff, clad in his scarlet suit with silver trim, wearing his wig and fitted out with his silver-hilted sword, Fleet left no question that he represented power, authority, and wealth. Fleet's father had made his will in 1728 leaving his widow, Elizabeth, the 650-acre plantation on which they lived for her lifetime, and then to his son, William. That will was not probated until May 1733, but in the meantime, William had died and his mother, Elizabeth, occupied the land until her death. By 1746, the rent rolls listed William Fleet's widow, Ann, in possession of a total of 950 acres, the 650-acre bequest and the 300-acre marriage gift from his father, Henry Fleet II.[11]

After the close deaths of his father and brother, Henry Fleet III became the senior male member of the important Fleet family. Unfortunately, he had little time to enjoy that position, for by February 1735 he, too, was dead. His unusual will left Banton in an extremely fortunate situation. The will offers not a single clue as to their relationship, for he did not even call her "my friend." He simply wrote, "I give and bequeath to Rebecca Banton my dwelling plantation with its appurtenances to contain two hundred and fifty acres contiguous during her natural life. . ." He gave her three horses outright, two mares, Conny and Jewel, and a gelding or stallion named Ball that was probably his own riding horse. Although he left his still to his nephew, he specified that Banton was to have its use during her life "without fee or reward." He made another provision for her convenience and probably for some additional income. Thomas Edwards, the weaver who rented Fleet's lower plantation, received use of

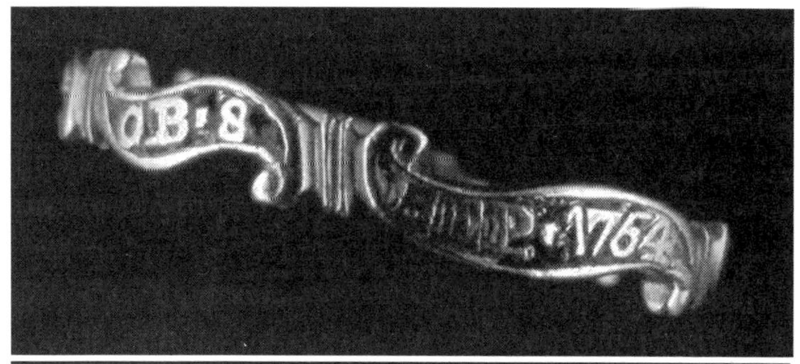

This 1764 mourning ring from Colonial Williamsburg's collection is typical of the type of rings devised in 18th-century wills. (Courtesy Colonial Williamsburg Foundation)

that land rent-free for 21 years, provided he would weave for Banton "eighty yards of Virginia Cloth per year."[12]

To assure that she had adequate labor to live comfortably on the land and in the house, Fleet lent Banton the use of eight slaves during her natural life, three men and five women. Furthermore, he provided the labor of an additional young male slave, James, until he reached the age of 24, and then charged Banton with the special responsibility to "obtain his freedom as the law requires."[13]

Finally, Fleet left Banton one-half of the remainder of his estate, mainly personal property, after the other legacies were distributed. Some of the other heirs named in the will were his mother, Elizabeth Fleet, his nephew George Fleet, his niece Mary Ann Cox, his nephew John Fleet, his godson Richard Edwards, Daniel Pugh, Davy Pugh, Thomas Edwards, and William Mugg. But by far his most favored heir was his nephew, Samuel Hinton, who was married to Elizabeth Brent, daughter of William Brent and Sarah Fleet, his sister. Everything that was left to Banton to use during her lifetime would go to Samuel Hinton at her death, in addition to the personal possessions, horses, slaves, still, and tract of land that Fleet had bought from Charles Kelly. Fleet made his friend, the Honorable John Carter, Esq., son of Robert "King" Carter, the trustee for his will.[14]

This substantial inheritance left Banton a woman of means. She enjoyed her position for the remainder of her life and faithfully carried out the obligation to secure the freedom of the sole favored slave, James Wright. Banton had a brush with the law in 1742 when she was ordered to appear in court for "feasting & harbouring negroes."[15] The charge was dismissed, but it suggests that Banton may have held a more open attitude toward slaves and free blacks than was sanctioned by the social mores and the strict legal code of the colony.

On October 1, 1750, when Banton was approaching 65, she made her will. Henry Fleet's will had already taken care of the disposition of the land and the slaves, so the disposition of personal property was all that remained for her to do. Her choice of legatees tells a great deal about her relationship to the Fleet family and about her own values. William Bond, a witness to her will and one of her executors, received a bed, bedstead, and furniture in the "Little House," a punch bowl, and a gold ring of 20 shillings value. She ordered a number of other mourning rings, each for 20 shillings. Richard Edwards, Henry Fleet's godson, received one as did Fleet's nephew, John Fleet, who was married to Mary Edwards, perhaps Richard's sister. William Hinton and his brother, Henry Hinton, each received a ring. They were the sons of Henry Fleet's favored nephew and heir, Samuel Hinton. William had married Ann Fleet, daughter of Henry's nephew, John Fleet. Robert Dudley's daughter, Ann, received another ring. Henry's niece, Mary Ann Fleet, daughter of his brother William, had married Robert Dudley. It is highly unlikely that she would have left rings to Fleet family members if she had not maintained a close and warm relationship with them through the 19 years that she lived in their midst following Henry's death.[16]

To another family member, Mary Cox, "Living in Westmoreland" she left "one Suite of Satten," possibly her finest outfit. Mary Cox was the daughter of Mary Fleet Cox,

Henry's sister, and her husband, Presly Cox, of Northumberland. All the remainder of her clothing she left "to be divided amoungst my negro Women." All the remainder of her personal possessions she left "to James Right who formerly Belonged to me," with the request that they be sold and that William Bond, one of her executors, have charge of the proceeds to give to Wright as he requested or needed. Thomas Edwards, Sr., Lancaster Clerk of the Court, and Samuel Hinton were the other executors with Bond.

The livestock, including 33 head of cattle, four oxen, 25 sheep, a dozen or more hogs and sows, and a horse were the most valuable possessions. She had one fine complete bed and another less valuable one. The other household furnishing, a large table, several chairs, and a chest, all seemed practical. The cookware, earthenware, and pewter were utilitarian and ordinary, but the proceeds surely served Wright well and afforded him the opportunity for a better life for himself and his family.[17] In this way Rebecca Banton showed herself deeply grateful for Fleet's generosity to her when she was a young woman of modest status. She returned the kindness in her generosity to a free black man who lived in one of the most difficult situations in colonial Virginia.

ENDNOTES

[1]FHCCRF - Parish Profile Archives. The story of Rebecca Banton and her family; Henry Fleet III, Banton's benefactor; and James Wright, her slave, have been painstakingly reconstructed through documentary evidence now contained in individual research files.

[2]Thomas Banton's possessions were modest, but by no means meager by standards of the day. He had 15 hogs, 15 head of cattle, and four horses. He had carpenter and cooper tools, basic cooking utensils, a modest amount of furniture, a sword, a gun and a pistol, hoes, some pewter, saws, and axes. Administration of estate of Thomas Banton, July 1698, Lancaster County Court Order Book 4:41.

[3]John Carter inventory, 24 July 1670, Lancaster County Court Order Book 3A.

[4]13 September 1671. The Lancaster County Court appointed three women to "search Anne Fford sevt. of Nicholas Wren & the sd. Anne it is charged, is with child of Thos. Banton." *Virginia Colonial Abstracts*, Series 2, 2:201.

[5]John Kelly accused Thomas Banton of killing his hog. Case heard 8 June

1687 and dismissed for lack of evidence. Lancaster County Court Order Book, 1686-1696.

[6]A Lancaster County suit of 14 November 1677 was John Skelson v. Susanna Marshall "the now wife of Thomas Banton." *Virginia Colonial Abstracts*, Series 2, 2:385.

[7]Will of Edward Banton, 24 November 1698, James Haines, Administrator. Lancaster County Court Order Book 4:53. Edward Banton was listed with one tithable in January 1700. His inventory was recorded on 2 April 1701. Lancaster County Will Book (1690-1709), 103. At court on 5 December 1700, James Haines swore to the noncupative will of Edward Banton. Lancaster County Court Order Book 4:129. His possessions as inventoried in April 1701 were far more modest than those of his father. Lancaster County Will Book 8:103.

[8]Petition of Rebecca Banton for possession of her estate, 9 September1702, Lancaster County Court Order Book 5:1; Judgment granted, 14 October 1702, Lancaster County Court Order Book 5:2.

[9]Dixie McCaig, "Who Was Henry Fleete?" unpublished research paper, FHCC; Harold S. Bowen, "Henry Fleete," *Northern Neck of Virginia Historical Magazine*, 40(1990): 4633-4642.

[10]McCaig, "Who was Henry Fleet?"; McCaig, "Where Did They Live?" unpublished research report, FHCC.

[11]Carter L. Hudgins, "Patrician Culture, Public Ritual and Political Authority in Virginia, 1680-1740," Ph.D. dissertation, The College of William and Mary, 1984, 233, 235, 239-241.

[11]Henry Fleet will, 26 November 1735, Lancaster County Will Book 12:358. Hudgins, "Patrician Culture, Public Ritual and Political Authority."

[12]Ibid., James Wright, Banton's slave, is the subject of another profile study in this volume.

[13]Ibid.

[14]Lancaster County Court Order Book 8:364, 369.

[15]Will of Rebecca Banton, written 1 October 1750, recorded 15 February 1754, Lancaster County Will Book 15:303.

[16]Inventory of Rebecca Banton, 16 August 1754, Lancaster County Will Book 15:353.

James Gordon
Planter, Merchant, Dissenter

The European settlers of Lancaster County included some Scots, French Huguenots, and an occasional Dutchman, but they were overwhelmingly English in origin and Church of England in their religious persuasion. James Gordon was an exception. He was of Ulster Scots background and was a Presbyterian dissenter, and yet he rose to wealth and prominence in his adopted Lancaster County. Later in his life he renewed the Presbyterian identity of his Irish childhood and youth and took a leading role in encouraging the Great Awakening in the Northern Neck and in building the first dissenting house of worship in Lancaster County.

Gordon, the son of James and Sarah Greenaway (or Greenway) Gordon, was born in 1714 in County Down in Ulster, the north of Ireland. Greenway was the surname of a mercantile family in Newry, County Down, in this same period.[1] James's father, James Gordon of Sheepbridge and Lisduff, County Down, and his brothers, Robert and George, were sons of James Gordon of Sheepbridge, gentleman. The grandfather, James Gordon, may have come from Wigtonshire, Scotland, in 1689.[2] He received a lease to substantial lands in County Down in 1692.

The grandfather's lease was confirmed to James's father and his brother in 1732. The lands that the Gordon family held in County Down with townland names of Lisduff, Cloughenramer, Derraboy, and Carmeen encompassed about 1,000 acres.[3] In a land where most residents, whether native Irish Catholic or Ulster Protestant, were tenant farmers on less than 25 acres, the Gordon family members ranked comfortably among the Ulster Scots gentry. Their lands would have been sublet to small tenant farmers, providing the Gordons a steady rental income.

During the 18th century, many Ulster Scots emigrated

from the north of Ireland to the British American colonies. They came to the colonies primarily for the economic opportunity of land ownership, but there was some religious motivation as well. By 1690 the Presbyterian Church was the established church in Scotland, but in Ireland the Church of Ireland, an extension of the Church of England, was established. As dissenters in Ireland, Presbyterians could not hold public office or attend university. They had to pay the tithe to support the established church while maintaining their own meeting houses and ministers by voluntary support.[4] There was a Presbyterian congregation near Newry as early as 1642. Robert Rainey was its minister from 1706 until 1736 and probably baptized James Gordon and taught him his catechism.[5]

James Gordon of Lancaster County was the eldest of four sons and at least two daughters.[6] In 1738, at the age of 24, he emigrated with his brother, John, from the port of Newry.[7] The Gordon brothers were certainly not the first Ulster Scots to settle in Lancaster County. The Reverend Andrew Jackson, minister of Christ Church Parish from 1682 to 1710, was actually a Presbyterian minister who had never been ordained in the Church of England. There is strong evidence that he was from Ireland.[8] There were other Presbyterians already in the Lancaster, Northumberland, and Middlesex County area. In 1708 the Scottish Presbytery of Irvine ordained James Anderson, a graduate of Glasgow University, as a missionary for Virginia. The presbytery would only have done this because it had received letters requesting a minister. Anderson served a congregation "on the Rappahannock," possibly in Lancaster County, but left there after a few months for lack of support.[9]

When James Gordon's father, James of Lissduff, died in 1753, he was styled "gentleman" in the probate of his will.[10] James, as the eldest son, inherited his father's land in Ireland and kept it throughout the remainder of his life.[11] The Gordon brothers came to Lancaster County as merchants, bringing sufficient resources to become established quickly and successfully in tobacco and in slave trading.[12] Like Robert

Carter and other great planter-merchants of colonial Virginia, albeit on a smaller scale, James Gordon maintained ties with merchant firms in Bristol, Liverpool, Whitehaven, and London, and had mercantile dealings in Antigua and Guinea also.

The Gordon brothers kept in touch with their family back in Ireland. In 1759 James Gordon recorded in his diary that he "Rec'd a letter from Mr. Jos. Taylor of Whitehaven, giving me an account of my dear mother and sisters at Newry."[13] His cousins Robert and Samuel Hening may have been members of a large family circle in his native land whom he convinced to emigrate. In his diary Gordon mentioned Capt. Robert Hening and Mrs. Hening, whom he called "cousin."[14]

Both Gordon brothers apparently prospered from the beginning and each married a daughter of a prominent family with important economic and political connections. On March 28, 1742, when he had been in Virginia only four years, James Gordon married 16-year old Millicent Conway, youngest daughter of Col. Edwin Conway. Conway was second only to Robert Carter in prominence in Lancaster County. He served on the county court, was an officer in the militia, and represented the county in the House of Burgesses.[15]

Millicent bore her husband four children before she died on February 2, 1748, at the age of 20. Only the eldest child, Ann, born in 1743, reached maturity and married. In November 1748, James Gordon married Mary Harrison at Bushy Park in Middlesex County, the home of her sister, Hannah, and her husband, Armistead Churchill. Mary was the daughter of Mary Carey and Nathaniel Harrison of Surry County, south of the James River.[16]

John Gordon, James's younger brother, who was based at Urbanna in Middlesex County on the south bank of the Rappahannock, did not marry for a number of years. In 1756 he took as his wife Lucy Churchill, daughter of Armistead Churchill and his wife, Hannah Harrison Churchill, of Bushy Park. Lucy was the niece of Mary Harrison Gordon, James's second wife.[17] Armistead Churchill's mother was a sister of Judith Armistead Carter, first wife of Col. Robert Carter of Corotoman.

James Gordon began to acquire land in Lancaster County in 1742, and he continued adding to his holdings for the next 24 years while selling or giving to his children some tracts on occasion as well. His first purchase was a two-acre lot "on the hill above Mr. Henry Carter's plantation where the road passes between the sd Henrys and the plantation of Wm. Stephens."[18] This purchase was the beginning of Gordon's patient and gradual acquisition of the former "Barford" plantation that had belonged to Robert Carter's friend and advisor, Thomas Carter. There at Merry Point, between the two branches of the Corrotoman River, Gordon built a substantial brick house with two rooms, a central hall, and a gable roof. A 1749 deed referred to "the Hill the sd Gordon's dwelling house stands on."[19] Although small in comparison with such houses as Stratford Hall or Carter's Grove, Gordon's house was one of the finest in Lancaster County at that time. It is important to

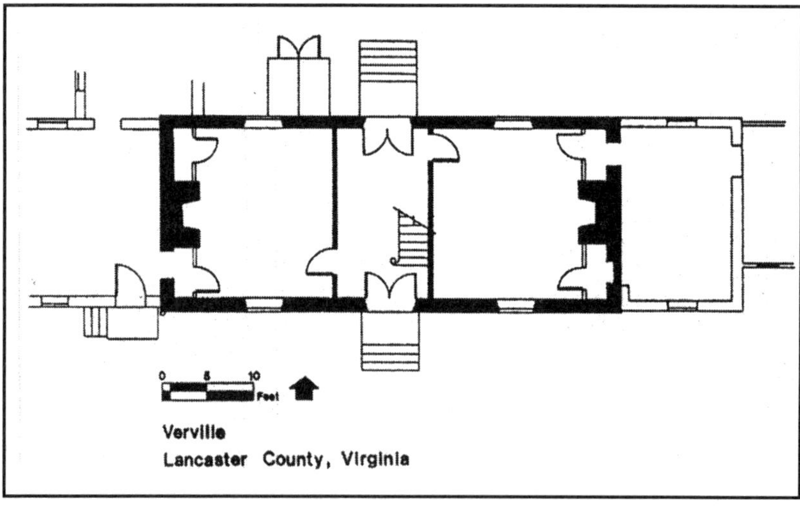

Although James Gordon was one of the wealthiest men in Christ Church Parish, "Verville" was only three bays wide and one full story in height. Through references in Gordon's diary, we know that the house was surrounded by many outbuildings. (Floorplan courtesy of architectural historian Camille Wells.)

note that while it was only three bays wide and one full story in height, it was surrounded by any number of outbuildings, including possibly an office and store, given references in Gordon's diary. So it was a really well-built and well-finished but relatively small house (two rooms on each floor) with quite an assemblage of "sentry" buildings around the site.[20] The house was known as "Gordonsville" during the life of James Gordon and of his son, James Gordon, Jr., but later owners changed the name to "Verville," which it retains to the present.

In 1743 Gordon purchased 70 acres from Richard Curtis and Stephen Mullis, and later that year he purchased 212 acres from his father-in-law, Edwin Conway.[21] Gordon's largest single purchase took place in 1745 when he acquired from John Belfield and Anthony Sydnor a 586-acre-tract in Christ Church Parish, which Gordon called Belfield's Quarter. This tract, a portion of which lay along Church Road, was superbly located on Carters Creek for a merchant-trader such as Gordon, near the ship landings and the glebe.[22] This area was commonly called Crab Point and Race Ground Point. Five years later, Gordon acquired an additional 50 acres near this tract from John Griggs.[23]

Gordon's other purchases were closer to his home. He added to his holdings nearly every year until he had acquired a total of 2,288 acres. Only three instances are known in which he sold land outside the family: 90 acres to Thomas Doggett in 1748, 100 acres to William Doggett in 1756, and 75 acres to Jane Ramsey in 1757. Both men were descendants of the Reverend Benjamin Doggett, an early minister of Christ Church Parish.[24] Gordon gave 395 acres to his daughter, Mary, and her husband, James Waddell, a Presbyterian minister, and transferred 180 acres to his son, James Gordon, Jr. At the time of his death in 1768, he owned nearly 1,800 acres in Lancaster County, making him one of the largest landholders there.[25]

James Gordon's economic activities in Lancaster County were varied, but among the most significant was the operation of a store at the courthouse. A well-run store at any courthouse in colonial Virginia could be a highly lucrative undertaking. Along with the church, it was a principal public gathering place for the community. Gordon's diary entries indicate that he visited the store frequently, took a personal interest in its manager and his health, and that he may have detailed one or more of his slaves to work there as well.

Gordon did not hesitate to use the courts to obtain judgments against his debtors. He was a plaintiff in at least 70 cases between 1742 and 1767, and a defendant in seven cases in that same period. In 1745, he sued Robert Anderson for 379 pounds of tobacco and was awarded 319. In 1746 he brought a trespass charge against Josiah Carter for "shooting hurting & destroyin a certain gelding belonging to ye sd pltf." The jury found for the defendant. The court required Gordon to pay each of his witnesses 25 pounds of tobacco for each day that they attended court in his behalf in the case, a total of 500 pounds tobacco.[26] This was a rare loss for Gordon.

Other suits that Gordon brought in 1746 were against the administrator of John Tayloe's estate for 597 pounds tobacco, against James Monroe, uncle of the future president, for 222 pounds tobacco, Robert Cornelius for 2,524, Gabriel Thatcher for 918, Abraham Gregory for 710, Robert Hunter for 390, Edward Sanders for 368, Moses Robinson for 283, James Galloway for 305, Robert Schofield for 349, and John Coats for 501. Gordon won all those cases. His suits against Alexander Power and Alexander Campbell were dismissed.[27] Suits that Gordon brought in the 1750s were often for substantial amounts owed him. In 1755, Gordon sued William Carter, who owed him 21,122 pounds of tobacco; Edney Tapscott, who owed 12,006 pounds of tobacco; and the executors of John King, who had owed him 11,577 pounds of tobacco. Considering that the annual salary of the minister of the established church was 16,000 pounds of tobacco, these were significant debts. Gordon won the judgment in each case, though not always for the full amount.[28]

It was an unfortunate but frequent fact of life in colonial

Virginia that small tenant farmers became indebted to the wealthier planter-merchants such as Robert Carter early in the century and Gordon in mid-century. In one instance Gordon sued the estate of one of his tenants, Thomas Howell, who had owed Gordon 50 pounds current money. Gordon asked for an attachment, or judicial order to seize property, on all the tobacco and corn growing on the plantation that Howell had rented from Gordon, as well as a young mare, a canoe, an oval table, two flagg chairs, a black horse, an old boat, a cow and two year-lings, a parcel of sheep, six hoggs, and some plank. The court required the sale of Howell's goods and crops to satisfy first his debt to Robert Harper and then his debt to Gordon. In another case of debt in which Gordon sued the estate of William Currell, the court ordered that a male slave who had belonged to Currell be sold at Cox's race ground in the county to satisfy this debt and two others.[29]

Gordon also entered a partnership with John Norris in 1761 in a milling venture on Fishing Creek [Brown's Creek] near Devils Bottom Road. Gordon put up half of the capital to build the miller's house, the mill, and the dam, and he was to have half of the profits from grinding Indian corn.[30] Gordon mentioned in his diary that "Wife went with me to the Mill, saw some fine grinding of Indian Meal." In September that year, Gordon and Norris agreed to have Norris's slave, Tom, as the miller.[31]

Gordon's reputation for wise financial management caused friends and neighbors to trust him. When Thomas Kelley died intestate in 1750, Gordon agreed to serve as administrator of his estate. Later that year, Laughlin Burgin died, naming Gordon and Dale Carter as his executors. When John Coats died intestate in 1765, Gordon and Dale Carter were named administrators.[32]

Although Gordon was primarily a merchant, he became more of a planter as years went by, eventually acquiring some 50 slaves to do the agricultural labor on his holdings. As with all planters in Tidewater Virginia, tobacco was the important money crop, but Gordon's agricultural practices, as indicated in the diary extracts surviving from the late 1750s, show substantial crops of oats, wheat, rye, and corn as well. Another activity in which Gordon had an interest was fishing. Diary entries indicate that he kept a seine in the river and regularly pulled in 100 to 150 fish, mostly rockfish and shad.[33]

By the time Gordon had been in Lancaster County six years, he had gained such a sufficient reputation for business acumen, good judgment, and success that he was appointed a justice of the county court. On August 23, 1744, William Tayloe and Joseph Chinn administered the oaths to Gordon, and swore him in, along with his father-in-law, Edwin Conway, Robert Mitchell, John Stepto, Peter Conway, Thomas Pinckard, Dale Carter, and James Ball, Jr.[34] Gordon served with diligence into the year 1747, attending a great many of the sessions, especially in 1746, but after that his interest flagged and so did his attendance. On August 10, 1750, Gordon was sworn in again as a Lancaster County Justice and took the prescribed oaths. For reasons that are not clear, Gordon appeared in court with his brother-in-law Peter Conway and William Downman, and all "refused to swear unto the Commission of the Peace for this County."[35] When a new Commission of the Peace was issued in June 1751, Gordon was once more named to the court, and again in 1758.[36]

Gordon also filled a number of other short-term public service positions. He was appointed from time to time over the years to test the weights and measures at Chilton's and Davis's tobacco warehouses. The Davis warehouse, built in 1731, was located at Ferry Point on the Western Branch of the Corrotoman River, near Gordon's house.[37] In 1746 he was named to take the list of tithables below Secretary John Carter's mill.[38] In 1747 Gordon qualified for a militia commission. In 1748 he was recommended to the Virginia Governor as Inspector at the Deep Creek warehouse.[39] The court detailed Gordon to find a person to repair the courthouse. For several years in the 1750s and 1760s he was named a surveyor of highways for the road from Mrs. Robb's to the Davis tobacco warehouse in Christ Church Parish.

In February 1746 Gordon and some others petitioned the county court to request an act of the legislature to unite the two parishes of Christ Church and St. Mary's White Chapel into one parish.[40] Some historians have suggested that Gordon may have served on the vestry. Because vestry records are missing for much of this period, the composition of that body is not certain. It is clear from his diary and from vestry records that do survive that Gordon had business with the vestry. Gordon's diary notes on November 16, 1761, that his overseer sent to his house for medicines for a dangerously sick slave "while I was at the Vestry."[41] In 1764 and 1765 the vestry paid Gordon on his account with that body. But his name never appears in the combined General Vestry meetings of the two parishes, Christ Church and St. Mary's White Chapel, in those years for which vestry records do survive.[42]

As time went on, Gordon became increasingly disenchanted with the established church, particularly its clergy. One example of this came in regard to a school that Gordon was helping to start and for which he engaged James Criswell as teacher. Criswell had attended the county court in January 1759 where he might have an opportunity to encourage parents to send their children to his school. Gordon noted that "Mr. Leland [the Reverend John Leland, Sr., minister of Wicomico Parish, Northumberland County] and Minis [the Reverend Adam Menzies, minister of St. Stephen's, Northumberland] behaved like blackguards in respect to Mr. Crisewell." Criswell got several students "though the Parsons did all they could against him, which seemed to make the people more fond of sending their children. I think such ministers should be stripped of their gowns."[43] The school met at Mr. Bell's house, starting with five children. Gordon sent his daughter Molly and her maid Judith to the school. When Shrove Tuesday rolled around, Mrs. Gordon went to the school to treat the children to pancakes and talked Mr. Criswell into giving them playtime.

With his own Presbyterian background in Ireland, Gordon

was ripe to join in the movement known as the Great Awakening that was sweeping the American colonies in the mid-18th century. At some point between 1735 and 1750, each of the thirteen colonies and most major colonial denominations — Congregational, Anglican, Presbyterian, Dutch Reformed — experienced this revival movement with its emphasis on the centrality of a conversion experience. Persuasive preachers and traveling evangelists, including Jonathan Edwards, George Whitefield, Gilbert Tennant, and Samuel Davies, carried an emotional message of repentance and salvation to some of the largest crowds ever gathered in colonial America. One of the first signs of that movement in Virginia was the 1739 visit to the colony by the Reverend George Whitefield, the prominent Church of England evangelist who could hold a crowd of several thousand spellbound by his preaching.[44]

A leading American exponent of that movement was the Reverend Samuel Davies (1723-1761), who came from the evangelical New Light Presbytery of New Castle and Synod of New York in 1748 to serve a congregation that had developed spontaneously in Hanover County in the 1740s and decided to affiliate with the Presbyterians. In his 11 years in Virginia before leaving to become president of the College of New Jersey (Princeton), Davies helped found several congregations, gained hundreds of members, traveled widely to preach, including visits to Lancaster and Northumberland counties, and founded Hanover Presbytery that served not only the evangelicals in eastern Virginia, but more conservative Presbyterians pouring into the Valley of Virginia from Pennsylvania.

The first application from the Northern Neck to Hanover Presbytery for a visit from a minister came from Richmond County in April 1757. In July 1757, a request came from Lancaster and Northumberland, to which the presbytery appointed Samuel Davies to preach three Sabbaths before spring. In the summer of 1758, a ministerial candidate, Henry Patillo, preached in Lancaster, and the congregation there sent another request to the presbytery for supply. In the spring of 1759, Samuel

Davies and his principal Virginia colleague, the Reverend John Todd of Louisa County, held a sacrament in Lancaster.[45]

Davies and other New Lights preached a message of repentance, stressing the necessity of a conversion experience. It was a theology that appealed strongly to the common man. Evangelical ministers and laymen alike eschewed alcoholic beverages, gambling, horse racing, swearing, and a range of other behaviors including ostentatious living. As they looked about them, ordinary Virginians saw that the gentry seemed to exhibit behaviors that the evangelical preachers condemned. Furthermore, the frequent companions of the gentry were the ministers of the established church, who became a special target of evangelicals.

The Gordon family members seem to have perched on the fence about church matters. They attended the established church regularly, both at Christ Church and at St. Mary's White Chapel. They observed religious holidays such as Christmas, Twelfth Night, and Shrove Tuesday that were part of the Anglican liturgical calendar but certainly not a part of Presbyterianism, and yet Gordon himself was often critical of the church. In September 1761 he noted, "Went with my wife to White Chapel Ch. It really seems mispending the Lord's Day to go to Church to hear such sermons as are preached there."[46] This may have been his obligatory once-a-month worship appearance to avoid prosecution by the churchwardens for non-attendance. After attending a funeral at White Chapel conducted by the Reverend David Currie, minister there and at Christ Church, Gordon dismissed the sermon as "a superficial discourse" and stated that Currie "don't touch upon real religion."[47]

On another Sunday late in 1761, Gordon absented himself from church, but there was no service at the Presbyterian meeting house. He simply recorded, "Blessed be God, we have comfortable books to read, as we have little or no instruction at Church."[48] One Sunday in January 1762 Gordon stayed home with his family, drilling his children in the catechism.

He reported proudly that "Molly said all the Shorter Catechism, Jamey 56 of the Larger and Molly Hening 106."[49] Until they could obtain a settled minister of their own, the recently-organized Presbyterians in Lancaster County had to depend on supply ministers that Hanover Presbytery assigned to visit them, or on lay leadership to read sermons and prayers.

Once the Presbyterian dissenters had determined to build their own meeting house, Gordon took an active role in making that happen. His first father-in-law, Col. Edwin Conway, had initially opposed the meeting house and had sought legal opinion in Williamsburg on the subject. Benjamin Waller, Clerk of the House of Burgesses, wrote Conway that under the provision of the Act of Toleration, the dissenters were free to build a meeting house, so the colonel dropped his opposition.[50] In September 1761, Gordon reported himself busy "making out lottery scheme to raise £300 for our meeting house."[51] In January 1762 Gordon spent a day "getting the lottery tickets in order & sending them to several of the managers." Gordon reported one day that he had "sold 26 tickets, tho' there are both open & hidden enemies to our lottery."[52] The lottery drawing took place from midday to evening on June 30, 1762, at the Lancaster County Courthouse. Gordon reported a large crowd and pleasing results.

Presbyterianism grew rapidly in Lancaster County. Gordon noted in May 1760 that the meeting drew "a pretty large company of the common people and negroes, — but very few gentlemen. The gentlemen that were inclined to come are afraid of being laughed at; Mr. Minzie endeavours to make it such a scandalous thing."[53] In November 1761 John Todd from Louisa County conducted a communion service at the meeting house. Gordon reported "about 70 at table, black & white." The only figures for communicants for Christ Church are those from Robert Carter's diary three decades earlier and from John Bell's 1724 report to the bishop indicating 60 to 80 partaking at communion services. The Presbyterians were already serving a similar number after only a few years' activity in the county. In the summer of

1762, 103 were served at the Presbyterian communion service. The following year 113 communed, 90 white and 23 black.[54]

The evangelical dissenters made a stronger effort to attend to the spiritual needs of slaves than most clergy and laymen in the established church had done. In late December 1760 a visiting Presbyterian minister, James Caldwell, preached at a night service in Lancaster. Gordon noted that "about seventy or eighty negroes were here."[55] The night service, and the scheduling during the week after Christmas, which was traditionally a time of holiday for slaves, gave greater opportunity for them to take part in a worship service.

The congregation called James Waddell, a native of Ireland, to be the first minister. Waddell was careful to step through all the required hoops, and he traveled to Williamsburg in April 1763 to take the oaths prescribed by law for a dissenting minister. In May, he read the Articles of Religion before the two local established church ministers, Currie of Christ Church and St. Mary's White Chapel, and Menzies of Northumberland, again as prescribed for dissenting clergy.[56] Meanwhile, work on the meeting house had proceeded. Gordon reported in February 1763 that he had contracted with John Atkins about making seats.

Gordon's interest in the welfare of the Presbyterian congregation's capable and attractive young minister went beyond that of a devout elder. Waddell fell in love with Gordon's daughter Mary, known affectionately as Molly, and eventually asked her father for her hand.[57] In the course of a long marriage, this couple produced a number of children who played a prominent role in the Presbyterian Church in Virginia as ministers, lay leaders, and wives of ministers.

The great evangelist, George Whitefield, paid a return visit to Virginia in August 1764, and wrote personally to Gordon when he arrived in Urbanna. Gordon and Waddell crossed in Gordon's boat to hear him, and they convinced him to visit Lancaster. In the Lancaster meeting house on Sunday, August 28, 1763, Whitefield preached to a large congregation, including Gordon's wife, who "would venture out tho' in such a condition." That evening, Mrs. Gordon delivered a fine son, Nathaniel.[58] On September 2, Gordon purchased a horse from Colonel Selden for £47.10 shillings and presented it to Whitefield for the continuation of his journey.[59]

Gordon did not rest after his work to obtain a good minister for the Lancaster congregation. He provided a school with a Presbyterian teacher, a meeting house for the congregation's worship, and extended his generosity toward the great evangelist, Whitefield. He also took a leadership role in acquiring a glebe on which the minister could live and farm, and in developing an endowment fund to help pay the minister's salary. Gordon noted in his diary in November 1763 that the fund had £600 in bonds.[60]

Gordon died in 1768, eight years before the passage of the first of several laws that disestablished the Anglican Church in Virginia. He is an excellent person with which to close this volume of biographical sketches, just as his father-in-law, Edwin Conway, was an excellent person to open the series.

Conway, a gentleman of the old school, although also a spokesman for the small planter, was firmly committed to the structures of authority that included an established church commanding the allegiance of the entire local population. Conway disapproved of the work of the Presbyterians in Lancaster and opposed their meeting house, right to the time of his death in 1763. Gordon represented an understanding of authority structures that would replace the established church with a generous toleration that led, ultimately, to freedom of religion. Although Gordon was a member of the planter elite, the opportunity to return to the Presbyterianism of his Scottish heritage and Irish upbringing in the heart of Anglican Virginia placed him in a leadership position for a new understanding of church and state. This new understanding challenged the centrality of Robert Carter's magnificent Christ Church in the life of its Lancaster community, but it also pointed the way toward a more tolerant and more diverse Virginia society.

ENDNOTES

[1] Sir Arthur Vicars, *Index to the Prerogative Wills of Ireland, 1536-1810* (Dublin: Edward Ponsonby, 1897), 205. Samuel Greenway, clothier, of Newry, whose prerogative will was probated in 1723, might have been James Gordon's maternal grandfather or great-uncle. There is another clue regarding Gordon's family in Ireland. When he died in 1768, James Gordon left by terms of his will £100 sterling to his cousin George Gordon (who was probably still in Ireland) and forgave the debts of two other cousins, Samuel Henning and Robert Henning. Perhaps the sister of his father or his mother had married a Henning, and these were her sons. Perhaps David Henning of Newry, County Down, who left a 1739 prerogative will, was Gordon's uncle and father to Samuel and Robert. Vicars, *Index to Prerogative Wills*, 227. Robert settled in Lancaster County and is mentioned in Gordon's diary, 16, 26 April 1759.

[2] When excerpts of the James Gordon diaries were first published, a descendant of the first James Gordon stated that James Gordon, the younger, of Craichlaw, Wigtonshire, of a cadet branch of Gordon of Lochinvar, was condemned to death and his estates forfeited "as a Presbyterian" causing him to remove to Ireland. The notes to the diaries offer no documentary evidence for this. *William and Mary College Quarterly; Historical Magazine*, series 1, 12 (1903): 12n. There is another printed version of the Gordon diaries. The most important early historian of Presbyterianism in Virginia was the Reverend William Henry Foote, *Sketches of Virginia, Historical and Biographical*. In volume one, originally published in 1850, (Richmond, Va.: John Knox Press, 1966), Foote includes portions of the Gordon diary, from January 1759 through December 1763. It is clear in comparing the two printed versions that BOTH must be read for the most complete account available. Each is an edited abridgement from the original journal. Foote's version concerns only church matters, but it has more detail than the *William and Mary College Quarterly* version. The latter has more detail on secular, family, and business matters concerning James Gordon.

[3] The source of Gordon family information in the *William and Mary College Quarterly* was Philip Crossle, a Gordon descendant living in Newry, County Down c. 1900. The manuscript of the Gordon diary has disappeared. Its last known owner was Dr. Henry Alexander of Hampden-Sydney College. The *General Alphabetical Index to the Townlands and Baronies of Ireland*, compiled in 1851, reported Lisduff contained 278 acres, Derryboy 1,032, and Carmeen 562. Cloughenramer may have had 756 acres. This source did not list a Sheepbridge. Cloughenramer may be the land listed as Cloghram by 1851, with its 756 acres. Sheepbridge is noted in the mid-19th century as having a fair. James Harshaw Diary, 7 November 1856, Public Records Office of Northern Ireland, D 4149/D/5 transcribed Emigration Database, (see below). A 29 March 1867 obituary in the *Armagh Guardian* noted the death of Charlotte Sarah, daughter of the late William Gordon of Sheepbridge, Newry. Central Library, Belfast, transcribed, Emigration Database, Centre for Migration Studies, Ulster-American Folk Park, County Tyrone, Northern Ireland. (Mrs. Samuel Townley, Esq. of New York)

[4] Good sources for the story of the Ulster Scots or Scotch-Irish include James Leyburn, *The Scotch-Irish: A Social History* (Chapel Hill: University of North Carolina Press, 1961); Jonathon Bardon, *A History of Ulster* (Belfast: The

Blackstaff Press, Ltd., 1992); and R.J. Dickson, *Ulster Emigration to Colonial America, 1718-1775* (Belfast: Ulster Historical Foundation, 1966 and 1988).

[5]"Newry Unitarian Church, 1578-1923 Interesting Historical Sketch." Public Record Office, Northern Ireland D 1079/M/1, transcribed on Emigration Database, Centre for Migration Studies, Ulster-American Folk Park, County Tyrone, Northern Ireland.

[6]"Excerpts from Journal of Col. James Gordon, of Lancaster County, Va.," appeared serially in *The William and Mary College Quarterly; Historical Magazine*, series 1, 11 (1902-03): 98-112, 195-205, 217-236 and (1) 12(1903): 1-12. The family information appears in a note at the conclusion of the series.

[7]Family tree constructed from entries in the Bible of Col. James Gordon taken from Nancy S. McBride, *Gordon Kinship* (Verona, Va.: McClure Printing Co., 1973), 137,141,145,146 in Christine Adams Jones, *Colonel James Gordon, Merchant of Lancaster County, Virginia* (Lancaster, Va.: Mary Ball Washington Museum & Library, Inc., 1983), 3.

[8]In his will, Andrew Jackson left money to a Presbyterian meeting house on Capel Street in Dublin. In addition, he left his Lancaster County lands to his brother James Jackson of Belfast, Ireland. Andrew Jackson will, 29 July 1710, Lancaster County Will Bssook 10:41-43.

[9]Minutes of the Presbytery of Philadelphia, 20 September 1710, *Records of the Presbyterian Church in the United States of America* (Philadelphia, 1841), 17; "James Anderson," in Richard Webster, *A History of the Presbyterian Church in America, from its Origin until the Year 1760, with Biographical Sketches of Its Early Ministers* (Philadelphia: Joseph M. Wilson, 1857), 331-442; William Henry Foote, *Sketches of Virginia, Historical and Biographical, First Series* (originally published 1850, new edition with index, Richmond, Va.: John Knox Press, 1960), 354-355.

[10]"A Calendar of Wills in the Exempt Jurisdiction of Newry and Mourne (1727-1858), in W.P.W. Phillimore and Gertrude Thrift, *Indexes to Irish Wills*, Five volumes in One (Baltimore: Genealogical Publishing Company, 1970), 4:168.

[11]In his own will written in 1767, James Gordon stated, "I give to my said brother John Gordon and to his heirs all my right title and interest of my land in the Kingdom of Ireland which was devised to me by the last will and testament of my father." Lancaster Deed & Will Book 18 (1764-1770): 105.

[12]Jones, *Colonel James Gordon*, 1.

[13]James Gordon Diary, 4 October 1759. *William and Mary College Quarterly*.

[14]Gordon does not indicate if Captain Robert Hening (or Henning) was a sea captain or a militia captain. Mrs. Hening, whom Gordon also called cousin, took sick at his house and died while her husband was away. Gordon consulted with her brother, Captain Spence, about where to bury her. Gordon diary, 15, 16, 17 March 1759. At the time of Gordon's death, the Henings were indebted to him. Gordon forgave those debts in his will written January 1, 1767 and probated on 18 February 1768. Lancaster County Deed and Will Book 18 (1764-1770):105.

[15]It is not certain who was Millicent Conway's mother. Gordon family records indicate that it was Ann Ball, daughter of Colonel Joseph Ball (1649-1711) and his wife, Elizabeth Romney Ball (c. 1653-1703) of St. Mary's White Chapel parish in Lancaster County. Conway married Ann Ball in 1704. She seems to have been the mother of four daughters, Elizabeth, Anne, Mary, and Agatha before her death. Next, most likely by 1719, Conway married Ann Hack,

daughter of Col. Peter Hack of Northumberland County. She seems to have been the mother of George, Peter, Hannah, and Millicent Conway. Millicent was the youngest child of Edwin Conway. Sources for these families include Ralph T. Whitelaw, *Virginia's Eastern Shore: A History of Northampton and Accomack Counties*, Volume One (Richmond: Virginia Historical Society 1951), 684-689; "Excursus-Hack," in Horace Edwin Hayden, *Virginia Genealogies: A Genealogy of the Glassell Family of Scotland and Virginia*, first printed 1885 (Baltimore: Genealogical Book Company, 1959), 226, 231, 234, 243-244.

[16]Jones, *Colonel James Gordon*, 2-4. Dates used here follow the current calendar with January as the first month. In the early 18th century, February was still counted in 1747, or sometimes written 1747/48.

[17]Ibid.

[18]Indenture between Thomas Carter and James Gordon, 20 November 1742, Lancaster Deed and Will Book 13 (1738-1743):312. See also 14 January 1743, Lancaster County Court Order Book 8 (1729-1743): 372. This Thomas Carter was a grandson of Thomas Carter of Barford, the close associate and legal advisor of Robert Carter.

[19]Lancaster County Deed and Will Book 14:243. The five acres Gordon bought had a house on it. Inconclusive dendrochronology dating on Verville was conducted in 2001 to determine when the oldest portion of the house was built. Unfortunately, an early 19th-century remodeling of the house replaced the joists below the first story. The date for those replacement joists was unquestionably 1809, however, the character of the brickwork and nature of the documentary records leaves little doubt, according to architectural historian Camille Wells, that Verville was standing by 1750. The other samples taken during the 2001 dendrochronology were from the roof timbers of the gambrel roof which has long been suspected of being a replacement roof for an earlier gable roof. That suspicion was, for the most part, confirmed, but an exact date of the roof's construction could not be pinpointed. Most of the gambrel roof timbers were tulip poplar, an unreliable wood for such dating techniques, and the rest were very squared-up oak timbers yielding incomplete samples. The only certainty emerging from the roof timber testing was the fact that the gambrel roof was added after 1775 and before 1785. E-mail letter from Camille Wells to Nancy Sorrells, 12 February 2002.

[20]Camille Wells, in her study of Northern Neck houses, includes a floor plan to Gordon's house. She emphasizes the point that at the time of his death in 1768, Gordon's land (which she calculated at 1,050 acres) placed him in the top two percent of Lancaster County's 289 landholders. His brick house, while modest by today's standards, was larger and finer than the dwellings of all but a handful of residents of Lancaster County. Camille Wells, "The Eighteenth-Century Landscape of Virginia's Northern Neck," *Northern Neck of Virginia Historical Magazine* XXXVII, December 1987, 4419-4421; and E-mail letter from Camille Wells to Nancy Sorrells, 8 December 2001.

[21]Curtis and Mullis to Gordon, 12 May 1743, Lancaster County Deed and Will Book 13: 328-329; Conway to Gordon, 8 October 1742, Deed & Will Book 14:1. Conway sold his tract of land to his son-in-law at a price well below market value.

[22]Belfield and Sydnor to Gordon, 14 August 1745 (recorded 14 June 1751), Lancaster County Deed and Will Book 15:44.

[23]John Griggs to James Gordon, deeds of lease and release, 9, 10 August 1750. Lancaster County Deed Book 14:294-5.

[24]Gordon to Thomas Dogett, 8 September 1748; Gordon to William Doggett, 24 July 1756

[25]FHCCRF - These deeds were extensively researched and the known holdings were calculated. Evidence was found of 75 acres that Gordon had purchased from William Shelton near the Great Mill pond and then sold in 1757 to Jane Ramsey. Lands Gordon may have owned outside the county have not been traced. See also Jones, "James Gordon," 12.

[26]Lancaster County Court Order Book 9 (1743-1752):90, 93, 104, 106.

[27]Lancaster County Court Order Book 9 (1743-1752):107.

[28]Lancaster County Court Order Book 10 (1752-1756):326, 345, 383, 409.

[29]Lancaster County Court Order Book 9 (1743-1752):109, 113.

[30]Lancaster County Court Order Book 11:303 (20 February 1761) mentions Gordon's purchase of one-half interest in the mill. Lancaster County Deed Book 16:121, contains details of the partnership agreement. This mill at Devils Bottom Road was near the present bridge on Rt. 614.

[31]James Gordon Diary, 28 September, 3 October 1761. *William and Mary College Quarterly*, XI, 4 (April 1903), 224.

[32]Lancaster County Court Order Book 9 (1743-1752):205a, 235a; Book 12 (1764-1767):93.

[33]For example, on 22 February 1759, Gordon reported that 125 fish came in the seine.

[34]Lancaster County Court Order Book 9 (1743-1752):36-37.

[35]Lancaster County Court Order Book 9 (1743-1752):206a.

[36]Lancaster County Court Order Book 9 (1743-1751):258; Book 11 (1756-1764):179.

[37]James Gordon, Jr., acquired the Davis Warehouse and the three-acre tract on which it stood from John Davis and his wife, Catherine, in 1783. Lancaster County Deed Book 21: 25, 16 August 1783.

[38]This was Carter's Great Mill, which John Carter inherited from his father, Robert Carter. Located northwest of Kilmarnock just off the present Rt. 3, this millsite was later called Kamp's Mill. A 19th-century mill on the site was undergoing restoration in 2001.

[39]Lancaster County Court Order Book 9 (1743-1752):168.

[40]Lancaster County Court Order Book 9 (1743-1752).

[41]James Gordon Diary, 16 November 1761. The fact that Gordon attended a vestry meeting does not prove that he was a member of the vestry, for he could have come to that group with some piece of business concerning them. Unfortunately, there are neither vestry records surviving between October 1753 and October 1759, nor any between October 1760 and November 1763. The vestry normally met in late October or early November to lay the parish levy. Persons who wished to press a claim for reimbursement might have shown up at this meeting.

[42]Tupper, *Vestry Book*, 11ff, 65, 67. Margaret Tupper's listing of vestry attendees shows the unlikelihood that Gordon was the only vestry member in the three years between 1755 and 1766 for which no vestry record exists.

[43]James Gordon Diary, 8 January 1759, *William and Mary College Quarterly*.

[44]The Great Awakening has been the subject of many scholarly studies. An early standard work on the movement in Virginia is Wesley Gewehr, *The*

Great Awakening in Virginia (Durham, Duke University Press, 1938). Two more recent and important studies of Virginia are Rhys Isaac, *The Transformation of Virginia, 1740-1790* (Chapel Hill: Published for the Institute of Early American History and Culture, Williamsburg, Virginia, by the University of North Carolina Press, 1982) and Joan R. Gunderson, *The Anglican Ministry in Virginia, 1723-1766: A Study of a Social Class.* See also Katharine L. Brown, "Presbyterian Dissent in Colonial and Revolutionary Virginia, 1738-1786" (Ph.D. dissertation, The Johns Hopkins University, 1969). Other useful works on aspects of the movement include Stuart C. Henry, *George Whitefield: Wayfaring Witness* (New York: Abingdon Press, 1957); Harry S. Stout, *The Divine Dramatist: George Whitefield and the Rise of Modern Evangelicalism* (Grand Rapids: Eerdemans, 1991); Sydney Ahlstrom, *A Religious History of the American People* (New Haven: Yale University Press, 1972); Bernard Weisberger, *They Gathered at the River: The Story of the Great Revivalists and their Impact upon Religion in America* (Boston: Little, Brown and Company 1958).

[45]Foote, *Sketches of Virginia,* I, 360-361.

[46]James Gordon Diary, 6 September 1761, *Sketches of Virginia,* I.

[47]Ibid., 30 November 1761.

[48]Ibid., 20 September 1761.

[49]Ibid., 31 January 1762.

[50]Ibid., 9 January 1759.

[51]Ibid., 22 September 1761.

[52]Ibid., 9, 15 January 1762.

[53]Ibid., 26 May 1760. William Henry Foote, *Sketches of Virginia,* I, 364. "Mr. Minzie" was The Reverend Adam Menzies, a Virginian who went to England for ordination in 1750, served Bromfield Parish from 1752-1758, and St. Stephen's, Northumberland from 1758 until his death in 1767. Gunderson, *The Anglican Ministry in Virginia, 1723-1766: A Study of A Social Class* (New York and London: Garland Publishing Company, 1989), 270.

[54]Foote, *Sketches of Virginia,* I, 369.

[55]Ibid., Saturday, 27 December 1760, 365. This was a "sacramental season" or communion service weekend. The tokens were customarily given on Saturday for those who intended to receive communion on Sunday.

[56]Ibid., 11 April, 20 May 1763.

[57]Ibid., 7 April 1763. "This day Mr. Waddel spoke to me about Molly." This can hardly have been a request for her hand, for at that time Molly, born in 1752, and named for her mother, Mary Harrison, was only 11 years old.

[58]Ibid., 26, 27, 28 August 1763. Nathaniel grew up to marry his first cousin, Mary Gordon, daughter of John and Lucy Churchill Gordon of Middlesex County. Gordon family tree compiled from McBride, *Gordon Kinship,* in James Gordon notebook, FHCCRF.

[59]James Gordon Diary, 2 September 1763. Foote, *Sketches of Virginia,* I, 369.

[60]Ibid., 18 November 1763.

Name Index